Alternative Shakespeare Auditions for Men

Simon Dunmore

A & C Black • London

First published 2002
by A & C Black (Publishers) Limited
37 Soho Square, London W1D 3QZ
www.acblack.com

© 2002 Simon Dunmore

ISBN 0-7136-6321-9

A CIP catalogue record for this book is available from
the British Library.

A & C Black uses paper produced with elemental
chlorine-free pulp, harvested from managed sustainable
forests.

Typeset in Palatino
Printed and bound in Great Britain by
Creative Print and Design (Wales), Ebbw Vale

Contents

Introduction

Shakespeare is demanded for audition a lot of the time. Unfortunately for auditioners, auditionees tend to choose from a very limited collection of characters and speeches; unfortunately for auditionees, they have to perform those well-known speeches exceptionally well to succeed amongst the incredible competition. Experienced auditioners will have already seen a brilliant Hamlet, Iago and Cassius, to mention but a few, against which we inevitably compare yours. If you use one of the well-known speeches at audition, unless you manage to hit that magic peak of performance, you are on an inevitable slope to failure.

Why do people stick to these popular speeches? I'm convinced that it's largely because they cannot face the idea of getting their heads round unfamiliar plays and characters written in obscure language. It's easier if you already have some idea of the character and play – from studying it at school, seeing a stage production or a film version. I estimate that nearly fifty per cent of *The Complete Works* are rarely performed. There is, sitting there unregarded, a great wealth of material from which the auditionee can draw. Why are they 'rarely performed'? Often, because they aren't as good as the famous plays, but they do contain material which is on a par with the greatest moments in Shakespeare. Sometimes, they are 'rarely performed' because the language is especially difficult (*Love's Labour's Lost*, for instance), or because the historical knowledge required to follow the plot is too much for a modern audience (the *Henry VI* plays, for instance), or because the stories on which the plays are based are no longer part of our common culture (*Troilus and Cressida*, for instance). Shakespeare's audiences would not only have understood the jokes and topical references, but also would have had a working knowledge of their recent monarchs. Greek and Roman history, classical mythology, religious practices, and the Bible would all be much more familiar to them than they are to us now.

Even the well-known plays have lesser known, but not necessarily less interesting, characters in them. For instance, Petruchio from *The Taming of the Shrew* is very popular audition fare, but in this same delightful play is also the relatively unknown (but ignored for audition) Hortensio.

The other fundamental problem for the auditionee is length. Most people don't realise that fourteen or fifteen lines of verse is often perfectly sufficient (providing it also conforms to the other parameters mentioned in the 'Auditioning Shakespeare' chapter). Just because the famous speeches go on for twice or three times this length it doesn't mean that they mark an 'industry standard'. I know that it is difficult for women to find 'original' Shakespeare speeches, but I'm afraid the vast majority of men choose from only about thirty different characters of the hundreds available. There are plenty of less obviously important to the plot, but just as well written, men with sufficiently long speeches. You can also look at suitable dialogue and edit it to make a single speech (there are several such in this book). Some people believe the idea of editing Shakespeare is tantamount to sacrilege. I think that this is ridiculous because there is no such thing as a definitive Shakespeare text (this is true for the vast majority of plays; most playwrights have alternative versions to that which arrives in print) and also in doing an audition you are performing a mini-play separated from the whole work and it therefore will lose some of the constraints that tied it in its original context. On the other hand editing dialogue is not necessarily simply cutting out the other person's lines. It requires time, thought and trying out to see whether or not it works.

Another thorny problem is punctuation. I largely worked from five different editions (Arden, New Penguin, Oxford, Peter Alexander and Riverside) of each play and in my researches to date I have not yet found any sustained section of speech which is punctuated the same way in any two given editions. I have tried to rethink the punctuation to suit the modern actor, and I have a pious hope that Shakespeare might largely have approved of what I've done – after all he was working with actors, not academics. There are a number of instances where some words also vary between editions, and when there is an important alternative I have mentioned it in the notes.

Line numbering also varies, so I have chosen to number each speech from one. There are only a few instances where this is true of the speech in the play.

I have written notes on everything that might be obscure, but not following the dictates of any one academic editor. You will find I disagree with them all in a few instances. I also looked up every unfamiliar or obscure word in the *Oxford English Dictionary*, which was incredibly useful in illuminating the language. Overall I have tried to help you understand the details of each speech in order to perform it, rather than to write essays about it.

I have also included a short character description for each speech. These are meant to help kick you off in the task of reading the whole play. They are inevitably sketchy and only give the basics leading up to the moment of the speech. I cannot stress too much the fact that there is no substitute for reading and absorbing the whole play.

This is my second collection of fifty speeches for men which are rarely, if ever, used in audition. There are plenty more.

Finally, I would like to thank all those who helped me by commenting on all these speeches before they were committed to print: Ross Armstrong, Seán Brosnan, Richard Chinn, Chris Loveless, Richard Ridell and Ben Warren; my daughter, Alix Dunmore, for inveigling colleages in the National Youth Theatre to assist; my mother, Alison Dunmore, for supplying me with tit-bits from her decades of watching Shakespeare in performance, and my wife, Maev Alexander, for her detailed and incisive comments on everything.

Male Characters and Speeches
Too Often Used in Audition

Hamlet (*Hamlet*)
Hotspur (*Henry IV, part 1*)
Prince Hal, later Henry V (*Henry IV, parts 1 & 2 and Henry V*)
Chorus (*Henry V*) – The opening speech, 'O for a muse of fire...'
Brutus (*Julius Caesar*)
Cassius (*Julius Caesar*)
Mark Antony (*Julius Caesar*)
Marullus (*Julius Caesar*)
Philip the Bastard (*King John*)
Edgar (*King Lear*)
Edmund (*King Lear*)
Macbeth (*Macbeth*)
Angelo (*Measure for Measure*)
Lancelot Gobbo (*The Merchant of Venice*)
Shylock (*The Merchant of Venice*)
Bottom (*A Midsummer Night's Dream*)
Egeus (*A Midsummer Night's Dream*)
Oberon (*A Midsummer Night's Dream*)
Puck (*A Midsummer Night's Dream*)
Benedick (*Much Ado About Nothing*)
Iago (*Othello*)
Othello (*Othello*)
Richard II (*Richard II*)
Clarence (*Richard III*)
Richard III (*Richard III*)
Mercutio (*Romeo and Juliet*)
Romeo (*Romeo and Juliet*)
Petruchio (*The Taming of the Shrew*)
Trinculo (*The Tempest*) – 'Here's neither bush nor shrub...' (Act 2, Scene 2)
Aaron (*Titus Andronicus*)
Malvolio (*Twelfth Night*)
Orsino (*Twelfth Night*)
Launce (*The Two Gentlemen of Verona*)

I have cited specific scenes / speeches against a character, where there is material elsewhere for that character which is not to often used. This list is by no means exhaustive – other auditioners will have other characters and speeches they've seen too often.

Shakespeare – The Actors' Writer

Shakespeare, and others, wrote for a theatre that had minimal sets and an audience that did not sit quietly watching – they reacted like a modern football crowd. (Conditions that they are attempting to recreate at *The Globe Theatre* on London's South Bank.) He had no lighting beyond available daylight and the occasional flare or candle, no sophisticated special effects and no modern sound systems. There was some live music and the occasional drum, trumpet, cornet, and so on, but the principle emphasis was on the power of the excitingly spoken word. And that's what Shakespeare gave actors: a brilliant vehicle, his words, that can really help the auditioning actor – also without sets, lighting, and so on. He also had incredible insights into how people 'tick', in a way that wasn't really generally understood until about a hundred years ago – famously through Freud and in the acting world through Stanislavski. There is a story about a man after seeing his first Shakespeare production: 'Hey, this guy knew about Freud three-hundred years before Freud.'

Shakespeare the Man

We have a number of tantalising facts about the real person, but not enough to write a definitive biography. One thing we are sure of is that he managed to make a good living out of writing and staging plays – he had a commercial eye for what would attract audiences. He looked for popular subjects and managed to avoid controversy by writing plays set either remote in time and / or set in other countries. (Only *The Merry Wives of Windsor* is set overtly in the Elizabethan here-and-now, and that doesn't contain any kings, princes and so on – people who if offended could be highly dangerous.) He didn't write contemporary satires to attract audiences – unlike Ben Jonson, his friend and nearest rival as a playwright – and he seems to have avoided any trouble with the authorities, unlike Jonson who spent time in prison. I think that because he didn't have any political axe to grind, he concentrated on the people in his plays rather than contemporary politics. Issues relevant to an Elizabethan are largely only of interest to a historian of subsequent generations. I believe Shakespeare's apolitical approach and his concentration on the personalities involved

1

helped to ensure his immortality. I'm not saying that he didn't write about politics at all, his plays are full of examples; but he didn't take sides. For example, though there is a lot in *The Merchant of Venice* which is anti-Semitic (shockingly so to a modern audience), Shylock, the money-lender, has some wonderfully sympathetic moments including this (from Act 3, Scene 1): 'I am a Jew. Hath not a Jew eyes? Hath not a Jew hands, organs, dimensions, senses, affections, passions? Fed with the same food, hurt with the same weapons, subject to the same diseases, healed by the same means, warmed and cooled by the same winter and summer as a Christian is? If you prick us, do we not bleed? If you tickle us, do we not laugh? If you poison us, do we not die? And if you wrong us, shall we not revenge?'

As a playwright Shakespeare wasn't working in isolation, he was a member of several acting companies, principally the *Chamberlain's Men* (later known as the *King's Men*). I'd like to suggest that *The Complete Works* came not just from one man but through the energy and ideas generated by groups of people working closely together. A man called 'Shakespeare' may have written a lot of the words, but he must have used their experiences to inspire much of the detail. And, knowing actors, I'm sure they had plenty of their own suggestions – good and bad – that were incorporated into the scripts we now have. This is the cradle, the sustenance and encouragement that nurtured the 'genius' we label 'Shakespeare'. Over half a century later another genius, Sir Isaac Newton, the scientist, wrote, 'If I have seen further it is by standing on the shoulders of giants.' I suggest the same could be said of Shakespeare and his plays.

Elizabethan England

Not only was he almost certainly helped by his actors, but also by the comparatively stable political climate of the first Elizabethan age. As often happens in his history plays, the threat of invasion (and vice-versa) was common in the reigns of Queen Elizabeth I's predecessors. This required armies and ships, which were a huge drain on the national exchequer and when she ascended the throne England was not very well off. Her immediate predecessor (and elder sister), Mary, was a Catholic. Elizabeth, a Protestant, was a ripe target for Catholic France and Spain – England's principal rivals. There were also a number of people in England who thought that Protestantism had gone too far and would have welcomed an invasion. However, the two continental countries were at loggerheads and ignored England until the Spanish Armada in 1588, thirty years after Elizabeth had ascended the throne. In the interim the English ships had been used for lucrative trade and exploration, thus building a strong economy, strong enough to fund the soldiers and sailors for the defeat of the potential invaders by the time of the Armada; and strong enough to support the social welfare of the nation. 'We were just in a financial position to afford Shakespeare at the moment when he presented himself' (J. M. Keynes, Economist).

Elizabethan English

Elizabeth was the most extraordinary woman, highly intelligent and literate, and she used her power for the sake of the people, not just for her own ends, as most previous monarchs had done. She created a nation, with the help of some brilliant chief ministers, which had 'a zest and an energy and a love of life that had hardly been known before' (Anthony Burgess). This 'feel-good' factor, that modern politicians yearn for, created a new pride in the English language. Previously, Latin had held sway through the church, over the bulk of printed literature and throughout the limited education provision that existed then. People spoke to each other in various English dialects, but the use of the language in written form was extremely limited. Anything important was written in Latin, with its very strict rules of grammar and spelling – but there were virtually no official rules of spelling and grammar for English. Witness, the varying spellings that we have of Shakespeare's own name: 'Shaxpere', 'Shogspar', 'Choxper', and so on. These arise because each writer of the name (or any word) would write down the sound of what he'd heard as he would like to spell it. The written English of that time was 'not fixed and elegant and controlled by academics' (Anthony Burgess) – it was a language ripe for exploration and development, as the sailors were doing with material goods in the new world.

All this lack of regulation means that it is very common for Shakespeare's characters to commit what we would now consider to be grammatical howlers, for instance plural subjects combined with singular verbs and seemingly non-sensical changes in tense. However, he was writing (in elevated form) in the way people speak and these 'howlers' often reflect the characters' state of mind.

The Plots of Shakespeare's Plays

The commercial playwright had to write plays that he could be reasonably sure would attract an audience and took his plots from existing sources that would be generally known and appeal to a paying public. Early works included: *The Comedy of Errors,* a free adaptation of a well known Roman comedy of confused identity and *Titus Andronicus*, which contains some beautiful language but is full of mutilation and murder. The three parts of *Henry VI* and *Richard III* are based on historical accounts of one of England's most troubled times which were finally resolved by acquisition of the throne by Henry VII, grandfather of the ever-popular Queen Elizabeth I – an event which happens at the end of *Richard III*. A modern equivalent might be dramatically to chart Winston Churchill's life from his 'wilderness years' (forced out of politics) to the triumph of the surrender of Nazi Germany.

Another aspect of this commercialism was the 'megabucks' that could be made by special one-off performances for rich patrons. For example, *Macbeth* was probably written for performance before King James I (Elizabeth I's successor). Banquo, one of Macbeth's victims in the play, was reputedly an ancestor of James; Shakespeare radically altered the available historical record to ensure that the King was not offended and included references to witchcraft, breast-feeding and tobacco – subjects very close to James' heart.

Some Significant Speeches in Shakespeare's Plays

It's not just the plots that Shakespeare adapted from known sources, he even adapted other people's words. For example in the court scene of *Henry VIII* (Act 2, Scene 4), Queen Katherine's wonderful speech beginning 'Sir, I desire you do me right and justice...' is an almost direct copy of what she actually said, according to the historical record. Enobarbus' famous speech 'The barge she sat in...' in *Antony and Cleopatra* (Act 2, Scene 2) is very close to a translation from Plutarch's *Life of Antonius*.

Shakespeare's Texts

Four hundred years on, it is difficult to be sure that every word in a Shakespeare play is exactly as he first wrote it. The problems with his play-texts begin with the fact that then there was no such thing as a law of copyright. That wasn't to arrive for another hundred years. Once a play was in print, anyone could simply copy and sell their own version with no royalties going to the original writer. Worse than this, once in print, other companies could put on their own productions in competition. So Shakespeare himself had very few of his own plays printed. About five years after Shakespeare's death, two of his actors John Heminge and Henry Condell put together what scripts they had into print: *The First Folio*, the first – nearly – *Complete Works*.

Amongst their sources were:

(a) Some of the original hand-written cue-scripts (just the individual actor's lines and his cue lines).

(b) Some previously published editions of individual plays, the 'Quarto' editions. ('Quarto' literally means the size of a piece of paper created by folding a whole sheet twice so as to form four leaves or eight pages. 'Folio' means folding that sheet once to make two leaves or four pages.)

(c) The memories of surviving actors.

None of these can be sworn to being entirely accurate because:

(a) Even the best handwriting of the time is sometimes hard to decipher. (We don't have any texts in Shakespeare's own hand.)

(b) Printing in his time wasn't entirely accurate. Think of having to place every letter, space and punctuation mark – each in the form of an individually-moulded piece of lead – into a frame that then went onto the presses. *The Complete Works* (with *The Two Noble Kinsmen*, which is not always included) total about 950,000 words, which is over five million characters; i.e. an average of roughly 25,000 words and 137,000 characters per play. Also some of the Quarto editions were printed from manuscripts written down during performances by people trying to 'pirate' the plays (often known as 'Bad Quartos').

(c) Sometimes actors have very accurate memories for lines they've said on stage; sometimes they improve on what the playwright actually wrote down; and sometimes, the lesser ones make a hash of the playwright's intentions.

Shakespeare probably didn't write every word anyway. There are at least four other writers who almost certainly contributed to what we now know as *The Complete Works*. It also seems to me likely given the circumstances in which Shakespeare wrote – for a specific company of actors – that they might well each have had their individual 'say' in the details of what their characters said and some of their ideas incorporated.

Further confusion is added by the fact that just one copy of a 'Quarto' or 'Folio' edition would be printed, proof-read and corrected, then a second copy would be printed, proof-read and corrected, and so on. Nobody knows whether these time-consuming processes were undertaken for every individual copy, but (to date) nobody has yet found two identical copies of *The First Folio* from the roughly two hundred and thirty that survive.

There has been such a mass of intellectual detective work trying to establish a perfect version of the text that I believe it is easy to get the impression of a super-human being whose works must be approached with over-weening reverence. Shakespeare was a human being like the rest of us. He was possessed of a brilliant feel for the use of language and how people really feel deep down inside.

I do not say all this to try to bring Shakespeare down from his pedestal; I say it to humanise a man whom others have deified. I don't deny that a nation needs her heroes, but I think that England has elevated 'The Bard' overmuch. True he was part of an innovative (even revolutionary) group that has rarely been matched for its degree of positive development. But, in order to bring life back to his works, nearly four centuries after his death, we have to feel for him – as a jobbing craftsman needing to sell his wares to make a living. We need to make his creations have real life, rather than being some too often regurgitated ceremony that sounds stale.

Finally, I have to add that without the presiding genius and humanity of Elizabeth I we almost certainly wouldn't have known anything of him at all. Periods of great art arise when the prevailing governments are prepared to invest in their nation's culture.

The Lives and Times of Shakespeare's People

It is obvious to say that life was very different for people in Shakespeare's time. To recreate his characters it is important to have some insight into how 'different'.

Birth and Death

It was quite normal for a baby and / or the mother to die at or soon after birth. It is really only since the second world war that such deaths have become rare in Western society. Even if the child survived the crucial early period, many only managed it to their teens. A working class family would aim to breed as many children as possible as workers to help the family's meagre fortunes. Many women, even if they survived the multiple births, were dead of exhaustion by their thirties. The men had the hazard of the frequent wars. Medicine was very rudimentary – if not grotesquely inaccurate – and too expensive for all but the aristocracy, so disease and malnutrition meant that people, on average, lived about forty years. You were considered grown up by about the age of fourteen and old by your mid-thirties.

The aristocracy were better fed and had access to what medicine was available, but their chances in childbirth weren't much better and overall life-expectancy wasn't that much greater. (Though, the real Richard III's mother managed to live until she was eighty.)

Contraception was available (in fact the first evidence of its use dates back nearly four thousand years), but was generally only used for illicit sex. (A pig's bladder for the men and half a lemon for the women, for instance.)

Marriage

In Elizabethan England the age of consent was twelve and it was common for women to give birth in their early teens. Lady Capulet says to her fourteen year old daughter Juliet:

Well, think of marriage now. Younger than you
Here in Verona, ladies of esteem,
Are made already mothers. By my count
I was your mother much upon these years
That you are now a maid. (*Romeo and Juliet*, Act 1, Scene 3)

Prior to this period dynastic marriages often took place at even younger ages – for example, the real Richard II's wife, Isabel, was seven when she married him. This occurred when important families wanted to expand their power and possessions by alliance through marriage – equivalent to modern corporate mergers. The marriage partners often had no say in the course of events designed for them.

Democracy

Although the idea of running England through a democratic system started to evolve some three hundred years before Shakespeare, the monarch was still very much in charge – if he or she was strong and ruthless enough. Parliament consisted of the nobility, senior churchmen and representatives of the general population. However, it wasn't a democracy as we would now think of it; more a collection of power groupings who used military muscle to get their way. The nobility had the threat of their private armies; the church (prior to Henry VIII's break with the Roman Catholic church) could threaten to call on military aid from fellow catholic countries. There were also representatives from each town big enough and two knights from each shire (or county) – but these people couldn't call on armies to back up a point, so they had very little actual influence on major issues. Right up to the latter half of the nineteenth century only a small proportion of the male population of the 'civilised' world was allowed to vote; a certain level of wealth and / or literacy being the usual qualification. In the United Kingdom women had to wait until the twentieth century to be allowed to vote.

Law and Order

There was no national police force and the legal system was fairly arbitrary – generally, favouring the rich. It was comparatively easy to commit and cover up crimes, if you were clever about it. It was also fairly easy to be arrested for something you hadn't done if you were vulnerable and someone with the necessary finances wanted you imprisoned.

Travel and Communications

The only forms of land travel were either on foot or using a four footed animal, the horse being much the fastest. The latter were too expensive for the ordinary man and consequently the majority of ordinary people would never leave their home town or village.

Even those who became soldiers would travel by foot. All this meant that transmitting messages and moving armies took an inordinate amount of time.

Even someone with exceptionally fast horses could only travel at an average of about twenty miles an hour, so it would take at least a day to travel from London to York, for instance. If you did ride far, only stopping to change to fresh horses, you'd be utterly wrecked by the time you got there.

Taxation

In medieval times the monarch really only needed taxes to pay for wars, his general living expenses came from income from property he owned. By Shakespeare's time the tax system was more extensive in order also to pay for the ever expanding machinery of government. The ruling powers would, arbitrarily, invent a tax to cover an immediate financial problem. The concept of 'fairness' in taxation doesn't really occur until the late eighteenth century and 'income tax' was first introduced in 1799.

The Church

The church had enormous influence on people's lives, the power of the concept of 'God' was all prevailing – with no alternative view on the way the world worked. All but the most widely read would not challenge the idea that in order to have a good 'after life', you'd have to conform to the church's dictates in this life. Science was only just beginning to question some of the church's teachings – coincidentally, the principal prime-mover of this 'questioning', Galileo Galilei, was born in the same year as Shakespeare (1564), though it wasn't until the year of Shakespeare's death (1616) that he was taken to task by the church authorities for his revolutionary ideas.

It is also worth mentioning that the other most wonderful publication during the reign of King James I was the English language version of the Bible, which was still in common use until very recently.

Education

Education was just beginning to expand. It wasn't just the wealthy who could learn to read and write. Free schools were opening up, paid for by more enlightened boroughs and open to children of worthy local citizens, i.e. the elite of the middle-classes. The lessons consisted mostly of Latin studies, the language in which most of the limited printed matter of that time was issued; and a drilling in of their duties toward God, the sovereign and 'all others in their degree'. The poor had to wait until the late nineteenth century for the right to universal education.

Sanitation

Even in London there was no such thing as main drainage systems; sewage was simply dumped in the street – to be carried away by the rains, when they happened. Plague was a regular occurrence and when it struck, public places such as theatres were closed to prevent further infection. Country areas, like Shakespeare's Stratford, smelt sweeter and people's health was generally better than in the then cramped and stinking London.

Light and Heat

Burning what you could acquire was the only source of these basics; there were no national fuel grids of any kind.

Primitive but survivable, England was just moving from an aristocratically run society to one where even the lowliest individual was beginning to matter – only thirty-three years after Shakespeare died, the English executed their king and parliament ruled without an absolute monarch for eleven years.

Within the confines of this book I can only briefly evoke a few basic aspects of life in Shakespeare's time. A character's life is not just battles and loves, won and lost. It is also the ordinary, everyday aspects that the dramatist misses out because they are not dramatic and don't serve the life of the play. In order to bring those characters to life you should find out as much as you can about how their lives were lived outside the action of the play.

Auditioning Shakespeare

Shakespeare acting – at root – is not different from 'modern' acting. Where it is different is in that his language uses words, phrases and expressions we no longer use; and (more importantly) the circumstances are invariably far away from our direct experience. It is your job (whether aspiring or professional) to steep yourself in the culture that influenced his plays if you are to perform pieces from them.

Many actors argue that doing an audition speech is a desperately artificial way of having their worth assessed. I would tend to agree but, however much you may hate them, you will periodically have to do them. Of course it's an artificial situation, but isn't acting about making artifice seem real? There are ways of making them work – think of Bob Hoskins in *Who Framed Roger Rabbit* and Steve Martin in *Dead Men Don't Wear Plaid*, both acting with beings who weren't really there.

I have 'road-tested' all the speeches contained in this book; it is now your job to research and rehearse those of your choice. You also need to prepare yourself for the varying circumstances you could be asked to perform them in. Think of an audition speech as a 'mini-play'; you are going to present a 'mini-production' of it.

PREPARATIONS
There are a number of things to consider before you start rehearsing your speeches:

Iambic Pentameters
Apart from the unfamiliar words, phrases and expressions, this verse form (popular in Shakespeare's time) is off-putting – on the page – to many people. I think it's a good idea to think of it not as poetry, but as verbal music: that is words and phraseology that people use when they have a real need to express themselves or 'touch the souls of others'. A good playwright not only writes good stories and creates credible characters, but also writes in language that will 'grab' an audience – language that has a music of its own. Shakespeare was a master of verbal music, along with Samuel Beckett, Harold Pinter, Sam Shepard, Edward Albee, David Mamet, Arthur Miller, Alan Ayckbourn, and too many more to mention. It is not so much plots that make great playwrights, it is their use of language.

Rhymes

Some of the verse rhymes, which can sound terribly forced and unnatural if you emphasise the rhyming words too much. You can't avoid the rhyme, but it's important to make it sound natural and not forced (as poetry is often read).

-èd

All the accent on the 'e' means is that you pronounce the 'ed' where you normally wouldn't. For example: we'd normally pronounce 'imagined' not sounding the 'e'; but if it's written 'imaginèd', you pronounce it 'imagin-ed'. Some editions miss out the 'e' if it is not to be pronounced and insert an apostrophe instead and leave it there, unaccented, if it should be sounded.

i', th', and so on

Some people balk at these foreshortened words. All this means is that you pronounce them literally as written. Listen to yourself and others in normal conversation and note how many letters we miss out.

Making Sense

As you start out on a speech look at the sense, ignore the verse. Look for the full stops, even if they arrive halfway through a line. Then, look at each clause within that sentence; then put that whole sentence together to make the sense of the whole of it. Then, start to put the sense of the whole speech together – still ignoring the verse.

Finally, look at what words begin and end a line of verse, they may have a significance that you haven't previously recognised. After you've been through all the processes of finding and becoming the character, the positioning of these words may add to your understanding of him.

'The multitudinous seas incarnadine' (*Macbeth*, Act 2, Scene 2)

In his musical on the life of William Blake, *Tyger*, Adrian Mitchell had Shakespeare appear as a cowboy, or 'pen-slinger': 'I can drop 'em with one line'. It's that turn of phrase (that has now degraded into the 'sound-bite') that makes Shakespeare's language so exciting. It is your job also to make it 'real' for the character – don't sing it, believe it.

Preconceptions

With the famous characters, forget any preconceived notions you may have, e.g. Hamlet is 'mad', Juliet is 'wet', and so on. Part of Shakespeare's insight is that he created (mostly) very real people who may primarily exhibit one aspect of human behaviour through the circumstances of the play; but, as in life, there's far more to them than that. Think how often you meet someone new and form an instant impression, then you get the chance to get to know them and find that there's 'far more than meets the eye'. The aim of this book is to steer people away from these too well-known characters, but the same kind of preconception can take over and dominate the performance. For instance, Cloten (from *Cymbeline*) seems like a classic 'baddie', but in his eyes he simply believes that he is in the right.

Selecting Speeches

Read through the speeches in this book and see which ones create sparks for you, without necessarily fully understanding the content. (Largely, ignore the notes and character description at first, these come later.) If the 'music' of the words feels good then you are over halfway towards finding a speech suitable for you. It can also be a good idea to read them – carefully – out loud, without any sense of 'acting' them. Then read the 'Character Descriptions' to see if the characters are appropriate to you (age, type, and so on) and assess whether it's worth going further.

Don't be tempted simply to go for ones with the most spectacular emotions – auditioners want to see real feelings not flashy melodrama.

Length

An audition speech doesn't need to be more than about two minutes long and can be shorter, which can feel too short whilst you are doing it. Interestingly, Shakespeare speeches often work better when they're even shorter; I think that it may be something to do with the fact that he packs so much into his characters – a few of his words can speak such volumes. Many people think that they're not doing enough with thirteen to fifteen lines of verse – which will probably last only about sixty to ninety seconds. Providing the speech has a complete journey to it, it doesn't matter if it's this short. On the other hand, you can lose your audience if you go on for forty lines. You may argue that there is no way you can show enough of your skills as an actor in such a short time. True, you can't show everything, but you can give a very good indication of your potential – like a good television commercial.

How Many?

For too many people the 'Shakespeare' is the speech they least want to do, and they strain even to get the minimum (of one) together. I think this is very silly. The best results I've seen have come from people who've worked on four or five – and even more. Especially if you are new to acting in his language (as opposed to just reading it), working on several speeches at once can give you a much broader insight into his world. And if you begin to fall out of love with one or two of them, you've got the others to fall back on. If you only start with one, you've got to start all over again if you become dissatisfied with it.

Verse or Prose

Some auditioners insist that you present verse speeches, so it is important to have at least one in your repertoire.

Read the Whole Play

Next, read the whole play (slowly and carefully), read a few commentaries and if possible talk about the play and its people with someone who knows it. It can be helpful to read a summary first and then read the play, but bear in mind that these merely sum up the major plot and what happens to the people, without giving much psychological insight.

When a play is completely new to me, I find it helpful to copy out the cast list and write notes about each character as they appear. Obviously this takes time, but it's extremely helpful to the process of getting under the skins of the characters.

On the other hand, don't spend hours flicking backwards and forwards to the footnotes to try to understand every line. A general sense of the people and events is all that's needed at this stage (and how your character fits in). It's important to get some idea of the flow of the whole thing – too much stopping and starting can make you lose any idea of the whole.

It is not sufficient just to read the scene a chosen speech is from – you won't gain proper insight into where your character is coming from.

The Immediate Context

When you've got hold of who your 'person' is, build up the stimuli that affect him: the other people (present and / or influential), the circumstances (place, time, and so on) – as well as the immediate provocation for the speech.

The Details

One of the fundamental keys to good acting is the degree of detail with which you imagine the above. For example, if your character is in a castle, it's not any old castle, it's somebody's home – maybe your character's own. Look at pictures and, if possible, visit castles that are preserved as they were lived in (ruins will only give a partial impression). Try to absorb the details of what it might have been like to live in one. (Touch bare stone walls, that'll give you a very strong feel for medieval living.) In short, find out (and imagine, if you can't find out) as much as you can about the 'ordinary' bits of the life your character might have led that are not mentioned in the play.

The Clothes

A supremely important 'detail' is the clothes your character(s) would wear. I'm not suggesting that you dress in period clothes, but to imagine the feel of wearing them. One of the principal omissions I see, is the sense of wearing a weapon, which many characters would do. Different clothes, including shoes, make you move in different ways.

The Notes

Begin to understand the details of the words and phrases of the speech through using my notes and those from a good edition of the complete play. (See my Bibliography at the end of this book for suggestions on this). Write out your own translation into modern English if you find that useful, but don't become wedded to that translation, you'll find it hard to go back to the original. It's probably best to write it out and then throw it away, so you get a better idea of the sense without becoming fixed on specific modern words and phrases.

The notes attached to some established editions can confuse with cross-references irrelevant to acting; they may be written 'about' the character, rather than for the person acting him. On the other hand, the notes in some exam text 'note' books can tend to over-simplify.

Research

When there are real people involved it can be useful to research what we now know about them. However, Shakespeare had a rather 'tabloid' attitude to the truth. The 'history plays' are based on real historical events (*Henry VIII* ends only thirty-one years before Shakespeare's birth), but, like many other playwrights since he doesn't always follow historical facts as we now understand them. Sometimes this is because the then limited historical research was inaccurate; sometimes it is because reality doesn't necessarily make good drama (common to all drama); sometimes (especially in *Henry VIII*) he couldn't risk the wrath of current sensibilities; and possibly, sometimes because he was writing too fast to research properly or he was simply lazy. Do research, but don't let historical inaccuracies confuse you: take what you can from history but the information gleaned from the play must finally be the deciding factor.

Learning the Lines

Don't sit down and learn the lines parrot fashion. In all this research into the background detail, keep going back to the play, your character and his speech, to check that what you've found out (and used your imagination to create) still fits with what's in the text. You will find those lines simply start 'going in' the more you understand them and the circumstances of them being spoken.

If you find that parts will not 'go in' by this process of study and absorption, then it is almost certain that you haven't fully understood what they mean.

Don't Generalise!

Because it's a speech too may people tend to generalise, and it all comes out sounding the same. In life very few people anticipate speaking at such length except in specific circumstances. You should think of it as a series of connected thoughts and ideas – the circumstances stimulate the first thought to come out as words, then another arrives and needs to be spoken, and another, and so on. Usually, at the beginning, you should convey the impression you don't know what you are going to say at the end.

Soliloquies

Shakespeare is famous for these and some people think that they should always be addressed to the audience. With obvious exceptions (the 'Chorus' and some of the clowns, for instance), I believe they are the characters talking to themselves – 'for' the audience. When we talk to ourselves in life we keep it private and mutter. In acting we have to communicate to an audience – this is one of the fundamental differences between the 'being' process above and acting. You've got to go through the first stage of 'being' before you can go on to 'act' your speech. Don't try to prepare the other way round.

It's useful to think of soliloquies as the character thinking aloud in order to try to organise his jumbled thoughts.

Difficult to Say Words and Phrases

If you find yourself consistently tripping over a word or phrase, try saying it in isolation – with a lot of over-articulation. Do this slowly and carefully lots of times and you'll find it'll become second nature to you.

Obscure Words and Phrases

I am still amazed by the fact that if the actor understands these – in his soul – the general sense will communicate to whatever audience is watching, and they don't need extra demonstration. This 'understanding' is not simply a mental process, it is a feeling for what the word or phrase means so that it becomes a totally natural thing to say in the circumstances.

First Steps

When you think that you know and understand what your character (or 'person') is talking about and understand their circumstances, start saying the lines out loud – aiming to talk to whoever is or are the recipients of the words. Don't think of it as acting; you are slowly beginning to become the 'person' who is saying those words – through the speaking of them combined with all your thinking and research. Take a line or two at a time, and go back over each small section several times until you begin to feel you are emotionally connecting. You should begin to see the circumstances really happening in your imagination. One (pre-drama school) student I taught was really getting inside a Richard II speech; suddenly he stopped and said, 'I can see those f****** horses!' I shouted, 'Keep going!' and when he finished we talked about his experience. The steady research and thought he had put in (over about two months) had paid off. After that he 'saw' those horses regularly when doing this speech, but it wasn't as shocking as the first time – just a normal part of 'being' Richard II. (Incidentally, he had no idea where this king fitted into English history when he started.)

When you are 'connecting' with your first line or two go on to the next, but use the first as a run up, and steadily on through the speech. (Please note that I still haven't suggested 'learning' the lines yet.)

I'm convinced that creating a character is very similar to the growing process from cradle to maturity.

Rehearsing Your Speeches

After you've done all this preparation you can start rehearsing your speeches, actually becoming the person saying those words in those particular circumstances. If you've prepared thoroughly, you'll be wonderfully surprised at how real, alive and exciting you can now make someone who was created four centuries ago.

Shakespeare's Advice

Hamlet says the following to a group of strolling players:

> Speak the speech, I pray you, as I pronounced it to you – trippingly on the tongue; but if you mouth it, as many of your players do, I had as lief the town-crier had spoke my lines. Nor do not saw the air too much with your hand, thus, but use all gently; for in the very torrent, tempest, and as I may say the whirlwind of your passion, you must acquire and beget a temperance that may give it smoothness. O, it offends me to the soul to hear a robustious, periwig-pated fellow tear a passion to tatters, to very rags, to split the ears of the groundlings, who for the most part are capable of nothing but inexplicable dumb shows and noise... Be not too tame, neither; but let your own discretion be your tutor. Suit the action to the word, the word to the action, with this special observance: that you o'erstep not the modesty of nature. For anything so overdone is from the purpose of playing, whose end, both at the first and now, was and is to hold as 'twere the mirror up to nature... Now this overdone, or come tardy off, though it make the unskilful laugh, cannot but make the judicious grieve...   (*Hamlet*, Act 3, Scene 2)

This is some of the most succinct acting advice ever given – three hundred years before Stanislavski (and others) were completely to rethink what makes good acting and how we achieve it.

The Speeches

Antony and Cleopatra

Domitius Enobarbus

Domitius Enobarbus came from an important Roman military and political family, and was convicted of participating in the assassination of Julius Caesar – none of these historical facts are mentioned in this play and he doesn't even appear in *Julius Caesar*. Shakespeare also changed other facts about him from the historical record available, and seems to have created an almost new character.

In the play, he is Antony's chief lieutenant, closest friend and adviser. In the early parts of the play he joins in the fun at Cleopatra's court, much to the disgust of some of Antony's other officers, and is full of 'light answers'. However, when Antony falls out with his co-ruler of the Roman empire, Octavius Caesar, Enobarbus expresses concern that the preparations for battle are insufficient and that Cleopatra's presence will be a distraction to Antony. His warnings are rejected and Antony is defeated in the subsequent sea battle. Initially he decides to stay loyal to his master ('though my reason / Sits in the wind against me'), but changes his mind when he realises that Antony is now making many more mistakes. When Antony hears of his friend's desertion he writes to him expressing 'gentle adieus and greetings' and orders that Enorbarbus' treasure (with 'bounty overplus') should be sent on to him. Now in Caesar's camp, Enobarbus begins to regret his desertion. When a soldier delivers the 'treasure', his regret turns to despair: 'I am alone the villain of the earth... I will go seek / Some ditch wherein to die; the foul'st best fits / My latter part of life.' This speech constructed from several shorter ones is the next time he appears.

He is usually played middle-aged, but could be younger.

---

3   *upon record* when recorded ('record' is a verb, not a noun)
4   *Bear hateful memory* Be remembered with disgust
5   *my villainy* (I have added this to keep the metre.)
6   *mistress* (i.e. the moon which was supposed to influence mental disorders.)
7   *disponge* drop (as from a sponge)
13 *revolt* desertion
14 *in thine own particular* so far as you yourself are concerned
15 *rank me in register* put me in its records
16 *master-leaver* runaway servant
     fugitive deserter
17 *He sinks down* (Some editions have '*He dies*'.)

Act 4, Scene 9 (Scene 10 in some editions)
Enobarbus –

Enter a Sentry and his company; Enobarbus follows
1   O bear me witness, night –
     Be witness to me, O thou blessèd moon,
     When men revolted shall upon record
     Bear hateful memory, poor Enobarbus did
5   Before thy face repent my villainy.
     O sovereign mistress of true melancholy,
     The poisonous damp of night disponge upon me,
     That life, a very rebel to my will,
     May hang no longer on me. Throw my heart
10   Against the flint and hardness of my fault,
     Which, being dried with grief, will break to powder,
     And finish all foul thoughts. O Antony,
     Nobler than my revolt is infamous,
     Forgive me in thine own particular,
15   But let the world rank me in register
     A master-leaver and a fugitive.
17   O Antony! O Antony!   *He sinks down*

Antony and Cleopatra

The Clown

The Clown appears only in this one scene and we know nothing about him beyond his obvious expertise with 'the pretty worm of Nilus'. This snake was probably an Egyptian cobra (*Naja Haje*) – such snakes are often used by snake-charmers.

According to the historian Plutarch, who Shakespeare almost certainly used as a source for this play, Cleopatra did a lot of research into poisons – testing them on condemned men in prison. She discovered that 'the biting of an aspic, the which causeth only a heaviness of the head, without swounding or complaining, and bringeth a great desire also to sleep, with a little sweat in the face, and so by little and little taketh away the senses and vital powers, no living creature perceiving that the patients feel any pain.'

Just beforehand Cleopatra has sent her attendant, Charmian, to fetch the Clown. Soon Charmian returns and a guardsman announces: 'Here is a rural fellow / That will not be denied your highness' presence, / He brings you figs.'

He could be any age you like.

I have edited the speech together from dialogue and used a few words of Cleopatra's.

----

3   *immortal* (He means 'mortal'.)
5   *of one* from one
6   *lie* (Also, 'lie with men'.)
7   *honesty* (Also, 'chastity'.)
    died (Also, 'experienced orgasm'.)
9   *worm* (Also, 'penis'.)
9–10 *But... do* (He has transposed 'all' and 'half'.)
10 *they* (i.e. women.)
    falliable (He means 'infallible'.)
13 *do his kind* act according to its nature
17 *forsooth* indeed

Act 5, Scene 2
Clown –

1   Truly, I have the pretty worm of Nilus here; but I would not
     be the party that should desire you to touch him, for his
     biting is immortal; those that do die of it do seldom or never
     recover. Very many have died on 't; men and women too. I
5   heard of one of them no longer than yesterday – a very honest
     woman, but something given to lie, as a woman should not
     do but in the way of honesty – how she died of the biting of
     it, what pain she felt. Truly, she makes a very good report o'
     th' worm. But he that will believe all that they say shall never
10   be saved by half that they do. But this is most falliable: the
     worm's an odd worm. [*He sets down the basket*] I must be gone,
     farewell. I wish you all joy of the worm. Farewell. You must
     think this, look you, that the worm will do his kind. Farewell.
     Look you, the worm is not to be trusted but in the keeping of
15   wise people; for indeed there is no goodness in the worm.
     Give it nothing, I pray you, for it is not worth the feeding.
17   Yes, forsooth, I wish you joy o' th' worm.   *Exit*

The Comedy of Errors

Antipholus of Syracuse

Antipholus of Syracuse is the long lost twin brother of Antipholus of Ephesus. When they were babies they were separated in a shipwreck. This Antipholus is brought up alone by his father. When the boy reaches eighteen, he becomes 'inquisitive / After his brother' and decides to search for him, accompanied by his servant, Dromio, who is also one of a pair of separated twins. Five years later they arrive in Ephesus (which makes him twenty-three at this time), where, unbeknownst to them their twin brothers live. All kinds of confusions occur, including the events that lead up to this speech. Not long beforehand, Adriana (wife to Antipholus of Ephesus) and Luciana (her sister) encounter Antipholus of Syracuse in the street. Adriana accuses him – her supposed husband – of infidelity and the two women insist the men return to the marital home. Antipholus decides to agree: 'I'll say as they say, and persever so, / And in this mist at all adventures go.' We next see the 'supposed husband' with Luciana who berates him for his behaviour and then suggests that he seeks reconciliation with Adriana. This speech is his response.

---

1   *your name is else* other name you have
2   *hit of* guess at
4   *our earth's wonder* (This probably a reference to Queen Elizabeth I.)
6   *conceit* understanding
8   *folded* hidden
     deceit ambiguous meaning (with the sense that they are apparently misleading)
9   *my soul's pure truth* (i.e. 'what I know in my soul to be true'.)
16 *decline* incline
17 *train* entice
     mermaid (Sailors were supposed to lured by the songs of mermaids, also called 'sirens', to steer their ships onto rocks.)
     note song
23 *death, die* (These words were frequently used with sexual connotations.)
24 *light* (1) buoyant; (2) wanton (He is implying that 'love' cannot sink and therefore cannot be stopped or 'drowned'.)
     she (i.e. 'love'.)

Act 3, Scene 2
Antipholus of Syracuse –

1   Sweet mistress – what your name is else I know not,
     Nor by what wonder you do hit of mine.
     Less in your knowledge and your grace you show not
     Than our earth's wonder, more than earth divine.
5   Teach me, dear creature, how to think and speak.
     Lay open to my earthy gross conceit,
     Smothered in errors, feeble, shallow, weak,
     The folded meaning of your words' deceit.
     Against my soul's pure truth why labour you
10   To make it wander in an unknown field?
     Are you a god? Would you create me new?
     Transform me, then, and to your power I'll yield.
     But if that I am I, then well I know
     Your weeping sister is no wife of mine,
15   Nor to her bed no homage do I owe.
     Far more, far more, to you do I decline.
     O, train me not, sweet mermaid, with thy note
     To drown me in thy sister's flood of tears.
     Sing, siren, for thyself, and I will dote.
20   Spread o'er the silver waves thy golden hairs,
     And as a bed I'll take them, and there lie,
     And in that glorious supposition think
     He gains by death that hath such means to die.
24   Let love, being light, be drownèd if she sink.

Coriolanus

Tullus Aufidius

Tullus Aufidius is the leader of the Volscians – enemies of the Romans led by Caius Martius (later called Coriolanus). Early in the play, the Romans attack the Volscian city of Corioles. Initially, Aufidius' forces gain the upper hand but the Romans eventually win the day largely thanks to Caius Martius' inspiration and personal courage. At this point, the defeated Aufidius has just entered and vents his spleen on his enemy with this speech.

Through the play Aufidius shows enormous respect for his enemy's prowess as a soldier and later welcomes him with open arms when Coriolanus is banished from Rome. It is also apparent that Aufidius is generally a man of honour and it has taken the bitterness of yet another defeat to push him over the edge into thinking of behaving dishonourably as in this speech.

He is probably about thirty, but could be older.

I have edited together two speeches, incorporated a short line of one of the soldiers, and cut a few lines at the beginning and end to construct this speech.

---

6   *Mine emulation* My rivalry

7   *Hath not that honour in 't it had* No longer has the honourable intentions that it used to have
    where whereas

8   *in an equal force* on fair terms

9   *potch* make a stab (with the implication of doing it unfairly)

10 *Or... or* Either... or

12 *suff'ring stain* painful disgrace
    by because of

13 *Shall fly out of itself* Shall change its (honourable) nature
    Nor Not

14 *naked* defenceless
    fane temple
    Capitol (The temple of Jupiter in ancient Rome.)

16 *Embargements all of* All restraints upon ('Embargements' is 'Embarquements' in some editions.)

17 *rotten privilege and custom* corrupt traditional immunities

19 *At home* In my own house
    upon my brother's guard enjoying my brother's protection

20 *the hospitable canon* the laws of hospitality

Act 1, Scene 10 (Scene 11 in some editions)
Aufidius –

       Enter Aufidius, bloody, with two or three soldiers

1   Five times, Martius,
      I have fought with thee; so often hast thou beat me,
      And wouldst do so, I think, should we encounter
      As often as we eat. By th' elements,
5   If e'er again I meet him beard to beard,
      He's mine, or I am his! Mine emulation
      Hath not that honour in 't it had; for where
      I thought to crush him in an equal force,
      True sword to sword, I'll potch at him some way,
10   Or wrath or craft may get him. He's the devil –
      Bolder, though not so subtle. My valour, poisoned
      With only suff'ring stain by him, for him
      Shall fly out of itself. Nor sleep nor sanctuary,
      Being naked, sick, nor fane nor Capitol,
15   The prayers of priests nor times of sacrifice –
      Embargements all of fury – shall lift up
      Their rotten privilege and custom 'gainst
      My hate to Martius. Where I find him, were it
      At home upon my brother's guard, even there,
20   Against the hospitable canon, would I
      Wash my fierce hand in 's heart.

Coriolanus

Tullus Aufidius

Tullus Aufidius is the leader of the Volscians – enemies of the Romans led by Caius Martius. Early in the play, the Romans attack the Volscian city of Corioles and win a resounding victory thanks to the inspiration and personal courage of Caius Martius, who is given the title 'Coriolanus'. Aufidius, after his fifth defeat at the hands of his enemy, swears revenge by foul means if that's going to be the only way to defeat him.

Meanwhile, Coriolanus, in spite of being a hero, manages to alienate the majority in Rome through his arrogant behaviour and is banished from the city. Deeply angry, disguised as a poor man, he seeks out Aufidius. There he offers to serve Aufidius and fight for the Volscians against Rome. This is Aufidius' response to this extraordinary offer.

He is probably about thirty, but could be older.

---

8   *grainèd ash* tough strong spear (made from ash; 'grainèd' means straight-grained which is stronger than a cross-grained one.)

9   *clip* embrace (This is 'cleep' in some editions.)

10 *The anvil of my sword* (i.e. Coriolanus, whose body Aufidius' sword has so often struck like the blows of a hammer sharpening a sword on an anvil.)

16 *dances my rapt heart* causes my heart to 'dance' in rapture

20 *target* shield

     brawn strength

21 *out* outright

22 *several* separate

24 *down together* fighting on the ground

31 *o'erbear 't* overbear it (i.e. engulf it; this is 'o'er-beat' in some editions.)

34 *am prepared* have an armed force ready

Act 4, Scene 5 (Scene 4 in some editions)
Aufidius –

1   O Martius, Martius!
      Each word thou hast spoke hath weeded from my heart
      A root of ancient envy. If Jupiter
      Should from yon cloud speak divine things
5   And say ' 'Tis true', I'd not believe them more
      Than thee, all-noble Martius. Let me twine
      Mine arms about that body, where against
      My grainèd ash an hundred times hath broke,
      And scarred the moon with splinters.
10   [*He embraces Coriolanus*] Here I clip
      The anvil of my sword, and do contest
      As hotly and as nobly with thy love
      As ever in ambitious strength I did
      Contend against thy valour. Know thou first,
15   I loved the maid I married; never man
      Sighed truer breath. But that I see thee here,
      Thou noble thing, more dances my rapt heart
      Than when I first my wedded mistress saw
      Bestride my threshold. Why, thou Mars, I tell thee
20   We have a power on foot, and I had purpose
      Once more to hew thy target from thy brawn,
      Or lose mine arm for 't. Thou hast beat me out
      Twelve several times, and I have nightly since
      Dreamt of encounters 'twixt thyself and me –
25   We have been down together in my sleep,
      Unbuckling helms, fisting each other's throat –
      And waked half dead with nothing. Worthy Martius,
      Had we no other quarrel else to Rome but that
      Thou art thence banished, we would muster all
30   From twelve to seventy, and, pouring war
      Into the bowels of ungrateful Rome,
      Like a bold flood o'erbear 't. O, come, go in,
      And take our friendly senators by th' hands
      Who now are here taking their leaves of me,
35   Who am prepared against your territories,
      Though not for Rome itself.

Cymbeline

Cloten

Cloten is the stepson of Cymbeline, King of Britain. Encouraged by his mother and step-father he pursues his step-sister, Imogen ('Innogen' in some editions). However, she has secretly married a 'poor but worthy gentleman', Posthumus. When Cymbeline discovers this he banishes the young man, apparently leaving the way open for his stepson to woo Imogen. Cloten sees her alone and initially she politely, but firmly, rebuffs his advances. He then starts to insult Posthumus ('that base wretch...') and she loses her temper and tells Cloten that he is not worth the 'meanest garment' that Posthumus wears. Following receipt of a letter from her husband she runs away to meet him in Milford Haven, a port in the west of Wales. When her disappearance is discovered, Cloten threatens to kill Posthumus' servant unless he reveals where she is. The servant gives him the letter and, after reading it, Cloten orders him to fetch some of Posthumus' 'garments'. Left alone, Cloten reveals his thoughts.

---

1   *Meet thee at Milford Haven!* (i.e. information from the letter.)
    him (i.e. the servant.)
1–2 (*I forgot to ask...*) (It isn't clear what this might be, but it's probably something to do with the scheme of revenge that Cloten is excitedly piecing together – like, how long ago is it since Imogen left?)
6   *noble and natural* naturally noble
6–7 *together with the adornment of my qualities* enhanced by my talents
7   *that suit* (i.e. Posthumus' 'garments'.)
8   *in her eyes* whilst she's watching
9   *torment to her contempt* (i.e. make her strongly question her previous contempt (for me).)
10 *insultment* contemptuous triumph
13 *knock* beat
    foot kick

Act 3, Scene 5
Cloten –

1   Meet thee at Milford Haven! (I forgot to ask him one thing;
     I'll remember 't anon.) Even there, thou villain Posthumus,
     will I kill thee. I would these garments were come. She said
     upon a time – the bitterness of it I now belch from my heart –
5   that she held the very garment of Posthumus in more respect
     than my noble and natural person, together with the
     adornment of my qualities. With that suit upon my back will
     I ravish her: first kill him, and in her eyes. There shall she see
     my valour, which will then be a torment to her contempt. He
10   on the ground, my speech of insultment ended on his dead
     body, and when my lust hath dined – which, as I say, to vex
     her I will execute in the clothes that she so praised – to the
     court I'll knock her back, foot her home again. She hath
14   despised me rejoicingly, and I'll be merry in my revenge.

Hamlet

Polonius

Polonius is the Lord Chamberlain to the King of Denmark and his master's eyes and ears as to what's happening. Contrary to Hamlet's (the King's stepson) view of him as 'a foolish prating knave', he is often very wise and perspicacious – sometimes even cynical and devious – however, he does occasionally become long-winded.

Here, he is talking with his daughter, Ophelia, and has been probing into her relationship with Hamlet. 'What is between you? Give me up the truth.' She says that Hamlet has 'importuned me with love / In honourable fashion' and 'With all the vows of heaven.' This is Polonius' response.

Although he is usually played middle-aged or older, I don't see why he couldn't be in his thirties.

---

1 *springes to catch woodcocks.* (The woodcock was thought of as a foolish bird which could easily be trapped in snares – 'springes', which is pronounced to rhyme with 'hinges'.)
2 *prodigal* recklessly
4 *extinct* extinguished
5 *a-making* being made
7 *something* somewhat
8 *Set your entreatments at a higher rate* Put a higher value on access to your favours
9 *Than a command to parley* (i.e. Don't simply grant him a meeting simply because he asks.)
    parley (This is 'parle' in some editions.)
10 *so much in him* no more than this with respect to him
11 *with a larger tether* with a longer tethering-rope (and therefore under less control)
    tether (This is 'teder' in some editions.)
12 *In few* In brief
13 *brokers* middle-men
    the dye the same colour
14 *investments show* clothes exhibit
15 *imploratators* earnest entreaters (This is 'implorators' in some editions.)
16 *Breathing* Speaking persuasively
    bawds (This is 'bonds' in some editions.)
17 *beguile* charmingly deceive
    This is for all To sum up
19 *slander* misuse
    moment moment's
21 *Come your ways* Come along

Act 1, Scene 3
Polonius –

1   Ay, springes to catch woodcocks. I do know,
       When the blood burns, how prodigal the soul
       Lends the tongue vows. These blazes, daughter,
       Giving more light than heat, extinct in both
5   Even in their promise as it is a-making,
       You must not take for fire. From this time
       Be something scanter of your maiden presence.
       Set your entreatments at a higher rate
       Than a command to parley. For Lord Hamlet,
10   Believe so much in him, that he is young,
       And with a larger tether may he walk
       Than may be given you. In few, Ophelia,
       Do not believe his vows, for they are brokers,
       Not of the dye which their investments show,
15   But mere imploratators of unholy suits,
       Breathing like sanctified and pious bawds
       The better to beguile. This is for all –
       I would not, in plain terms, from this time forth
       Have you so slander any moment leisure
20   As to give words or talk with the Lord Hamlet.
21   Look to 't, I charge you. Come your ways.

Hamlet

Claudius

Claudius, King of Denmark, married his brother's wife (Gertrude) a month after his predecessor's sudden death. Hamlet is told by the ghost of his father that he was murdered by Claudius, who was already having an affair with Gertrude. Hamlet, unsurprisingly, behaves very strangely towards everyone as he contemplates how to carry out his promise (to his father's ghost) of revenge. After a series of incidents, including Hamlet's staging of a play which re-enacts Claudius' crime, Gertrude asks her son to come to talk with her in private. Hidden behind a curtain, Polonius (a close adviser to Claudius) is listening to them. When Hamlet seems to threaten his mother, Polonius cries out for help and Hamlet kills him. Claudius hurriedly arranges for his burial and sends his stepson to England ('with fiery quickness'), where he has arranged for the 'present death of Hamlet.'

In this scene, Ophelia (Polonius' daughter and once loved by Hamlet) speaks (and sings) apparent nonsense to Gertrude, and when Claudius arrives her theme changes to seduction and betrayal. Suddenly, she leaves talking distractedly of burial and that 'My brother shall know of it.' Claudius orders attendants to follow her and is left alone with Gertrude.

It is important to remember that Gertrude wasn't party to her late husband's murder and doesn't know what fate Claudius has arranged for her son. It is also important for Claudius to convince his wife that he is trying to protect Hamlet.

He is generally played middle-aged but could be in his mid-thirties.

---

2   *and now behold!* (This phrase is not in some editions.)

6   *author* originator (through his killing of Polonius)

7   *remove* removal
     muddied confused

8   *Thick and unwholesome* Agitated and suspicious (like a pool of water when it is stirred up)
     whispers malicious gossip

9   *we* (i.e. Claudius himself – the royal 'we')
     done but greenly have acted naively

10   *In hugger-mugger to inter him* In burying him secretly and quickly

12   *pictures* (i.e. without an inner 'self' or soul.)

13   *as much containing* just as important

15   *Feeds on his wonder* Driven by his bewilderment (at the sudden turn of events)
     in clouds mystified by all the rumours he's heard

16   *wants not buzzers* doesn't lack rumour-mongers

18   *Wherein necessity* In these circumstances
     of matter beggar'd short of facts

19   *Will nothing stick our person to arraign* People won't hesitate to accuse me personally
     ('person' is 'persons' in some editions.)

20   *In ear and ear* (i.e. one after another.)

21   *murd'ring-piece* (A type of cannon which scattered shot in many directions, hitting many men at the same time.)

22   *superfluous death* (Since one 'shot' would be sufficient to kill me.)

Act 4, Scene 5
Claudius –

1   O, this is the poison of deep grief! It springs
        All from her father's death – and now behold!
        O Gertrude, Gertrude,
        When sorrows come, they come not single spies,
5   But in battalions. First, her father slain;
        Next, your son gone, and he most violent author
        Of his own just remove; the people muddied,
        Thick and unwholesome in their thoughts and whispers
        For good Polonius' death; and we have done but greenly
10   In hugger-mugger to inter him; poor Ophelia
        Divided from herself and her fair judgement,
        Without the which we are pictures or mere beasts;
        Last, and as much containing as all these,
        Her brother is in secret come from France,
15   Feeds on his wonder, keeps himself in clouds,
        And wants not buzzers to infect his ear
        With pestilent speeches of his father's death;
        Wherein necessity, of matter beggared,
        Will nothing stick our person to arraign
20   In ear and ear. O my dear Gertrude, this,
        Like to a murd'ring-piece, in many places
22   Gives me superfluous death.

Henry IV, part 1

Gadshill

Gadshill is a professional thief. Earlier in the play, Sir John Falstaff tells Prince Hal (later Henry V) and Poins (Hal's friend) that Gadshill is planning a robbery, 'tomorrow morning by four o'clock early', which they will all join. He also describes him as 'the most omnipotent villain that ever cried "Stand!"' Later that night, Gadshill himself first appears – in an inn near the site of the planned robbery. There he learns of some travellers carrying valuables. He questions the chamberlain of the inn (a servant who looked after the guests' rooms and obviously an old acquaintance) who gives him more precise details of the travellers' movements, but who also goes on to mention the penalty if Gadshill gets caught: the hangman. This speech is Gadshill's response.

'Gadshill' was probably named after Gad's Hill a place just outside Rochester in Kent and notorious for robberies.

He could be any age above about mid-twenties.

---

4   *Troyans* good companions (of mine; this is 'Trojans' in some editions)
    sport' sport's
5   *the profession* (i.e. of thief.)
6   *credit'* credit's
7   *joined* associated
    foot-landrakers thieves (working on foot – footpads)
7–8 *long-staff sixpenny strikers* (i.e. petty thieves, who will rob a man for sixpence – using a 'long-staff' as their only weapon.)
8–9 *mustachio purple-hued maltworms* moustached, purple-faced (i.e. habitual), drinkers
9   *but with* but those with
10 *burgomasters* governors
    'oyez'-ers (i.e. Town Criers, whose call to attention is 'Oyez!' ('Hear, ye!'). This is variously, 'oney'rs', 'onyers' or 'O-yeas' in other editions.)
    hold in stick determinedly together
12 *zounds* (A mild oath, short for 'God's wounds'.)
13 *commonwealth* public good
15 *boots* spoils

Act 2, Scene 1
Gadshill –

1   What talkest thou to me of the hangman? If I hang, I'll make
a fat pair of gallows; for if I hang, old Sir John hangs with me,
and thou knowest he's no starveling. Tut, there are other
Troyans that thou dreamest not of, the which for sport' sake
5   are content to do the profession some grace, that would, if
matters should be looked into, for their own credit' sake
make all whole. I am joined with no foot-landrakers, no long-
staff sixpenny strikers, none of these mad mustachio purple-
hued maltworms, but with nobility and tranquillity,
10   burgomasters and great 'oyez'-ers; such as can hold in, such
as will strike sooner than speak, and speak sooner than drink,
and drink sooner than pray. And yet, zounds, I lie, for they
pray continually to their saint the commonwealth; or rather,
not pray to her, but prey on her; for they ride up and down
15   on her and make her their boots.

Henry IV, part 2

Morton

Morton is a retainer of the Earl of Northumberland, principal opponent of King Henry in *Henry IV, part 1* – at the end of that play the Earl's forces are defeated at the battle of Shrewsbury. At the beginning of this play, the old Earl is given confusing and contradictory reports of how the battle progressed, and of the fate of his son, Harry Percy. Morton, an eyewitness to the battle, then arrives – before he even speaks the Earl comments: 'Yea, this man's brow, like to a title-leaf, / Fortells the nature of a tragic volume.' However, much as he wants definite news from Morton, the Earl does not want it to involve the death of his son – 'say not that Percy's dead.' Another Lord comments, 'I cannot think, my lord, your son is dead.' Morton then gives the full story with this speech.

Morton only appears in this scene and we know nothing about him – he could be almost any age you like.

All the events that he describes in this speech take place in the last three scenes of *Henry IV, part 1*.

---

4   *Rend'ring faint quittance* Offering little resistance
     out-breathed out of breath
5   *Harry Monmouth* (Eldest son of Henry IV and later Henry V.)
8   *In few* In short
10   *Being bruited once* As soon as it was reported
     best-tempered courage in most highly-motivated of (Steel was 'tempered' to make it strong but flexible, especially for swords.)
13   *abated* weakened
16   *Upon enforcement* Once forced into motion
19   *aim* target
24   *th' appearance of* people appearing to be
25   *Gan* Began to
     vail his stomach lose his courage
     grace excuse (by his own example)
30   *conduct* command
     Lancaster (One of Henry IV's younger sons.)
31   *at* in
     Westmorland (The Earl of Westmorland, one of Henry IV's principle allies.)

Act 1, Scene 1
Morton –

[*To Northumberland*]

1   I am sorry I should force you to believe
That which I would to God I had not seen;
But these mine eyes saw him in bloody state,
Rend'ring faint quittance, wearied and out-breathed,
5   To Harry Monmouth, whose swift wrath beat down
The never-daunted Percy to the earth,
From whence with life he never more sprung up.
In few, his death, whose spirit lent a fire
Even to the dullest peasant in his camp,
10   Being bruited once, took fire and heat away
From the best-tempered courage in his troops;
For from his metal was his party steeled,
Which once in him abated, all the rest
Turned on themselves, like dull and heavy lead;
15   And, as the thing that's heavy in itself
Upon enforcement flies with greatest speed,
So did our men, heavy in Hotspur's loss,
Lend to this weight such lightness with their fear
That arrows fled not swifter toward their aim
20   Than did our soldiers, aiming at their safety,
Fly from the field. Then was that noble Worcester
Too soon ta'en prisoner; and that furious Scot
The bloody Douglas, whose well-labouring sword
Had three times slain th' appearance of the King,
25   Gan vail his stomach, and did grace the shame
Of those that turned their backs, and in his flight,
Stumbling in fear, was took. The sum of all
Is that the King hath won, and hath sent out
A speedy power to encounter you, my lord,
30   Under the conduct of young Lancaster
And Westmorland. This is the news at full.

Henry V

The Constable of France

The Constable of France, Charles Delabret (d. 1415) is the commander of the French king's army. Earlier in the play, the Dauphin speaks of King Henry V as 'a vain, giddy, shallow, humorous youth' and maintains that the French shouldn't worry about him and his invading army. The Constable cautions him: 'You are too much mistaken in this king.' He is later proved correct as the English successfully advance through France in spite of the superiority of the French forces. The French king orders a massive assault to stop the English and the two armies face each other at Agincourt, a village in northern France. The night before the battle the Constable jokes confidently with three French aristocrats who are supporting the king. The following morning a messenger arrives to tell them that the English are ready for battle. This speech is his response.

There are very few clues to his character beyond a slight sense of caution in the banter, the night before the battle. He is usually played middle-aged but could be younger.

---

3   *fair show* splendid appearance
4   *shales* shells (synonymous with 'husks')
7   *curtle-axe* cutlass (A short sword designed for cutting rather than thrusting.)
11 *positive 'gainst all exceptions* indisputably true
12 *superfluous* excessive (to requirements in these circumstances)
14 *squares of battle* square formations of soldiers (ready for battle)
      enough (This is 'enow' in some editions.)
15 *hilding* good-for-nothing
16 *mountain's basis* by nearby mountain's foot
17 *idle speculation* inactive observation
18 *must not* (i.e. must not allow us to do.)
      What's to say? What else needs to be said?
21 *tucket sonance* resounding flourish
      note signal
22 *dare the field* dazzle the battlefield (with supreme confidence; the French wore glittering armour.)
23 *England* (i.e. King Henry V.)
      couch cower

Act 4, Scene 2
Constable –

1   To horse, you gallant princes, straight to horse!
        Do but behold yon poor and starvèd band,
        And your fair show shall suck away their souls,
        Leaving them but the shales and husks of men.
5   There is not work enough for all our hands,
        Scarce blood enough in all their sickly veins
        To give each naked curtal-axe a stain
        That our French gallants shall today draw out,
        And sheathe for lack of sport. Let us but blow on them,
10   The vapour of our valour will o'erturn them.
        'Tis positive 'gainst all exceptions, lords,
        That our superfluous lackeys and our peasants,
        Who in unnecessary action swarm
        About our squares of battle, were enough
15   To purge this field of such a hilding foe;
        Though we upon this mountain's basis by
        Took stand for idle speculation,
        But that our honours must not. What's to say?
        A very little little let us do
20   And all is done. Then let the trumpets sound
        The tucket sonance and the note to mount;
        For our approach shall so much dare the field
23   That England shall couch down in fear and yield.

Henry VI, part 1

Lord John Talbot

Lord John Talbot (c. 1388–1453) was the principal English military hero in the latter years of 'The Hundred Years War' between England and France. The English were in the ascendancy after Henry V's victory at Agincourt in 1415; but he died in 1422 and his son, Henry VI, was still a baby and the country was run by a fractious nobility.

The English led by the Earl of Salisbury are besieging the town of Orléans; he, Talbot and others are in an observation tower which has just been struck by a French cannonball. Salisbury and another man are badly injured. This speech is Talbot's reaction in the immediate aftermath.

Historically, he was about forty at this time, but I don't see why he cannot be played younger – providing there's a sense of a battle-hardened soldier.

I have cut several lines which refer to the other injured man, which could be confusing in audition. You could cut the last two lines.

---

1   *crossed* afflicted
3   *How far'st thou* How do you fare
     mirror of example to
     martial fighting
9   *trump* trumpet (Often used to send battle-signals, as were drums.)
10   *leave* cease from
15   *wants* lacks
16   *whiles* until
18   *As who* As one who
20   *Plantagenet* (Salisbury was descended from Edward I, who was one of the 'Plantagenet' kings of England.)
     and like thee, Nero (This is 'Nero-like' in some editions.)
21   *Play on the lute* (The Roman Emperor was supposed to have played the lute, sitting in a tower to watch, whilst Rome burned.)
22   *only in my name* at the sound of my name

Act 1, Scene 4 (Scene 6 in some editions)
Talbot –

1	What chance is this that suddenly hath crossed us?
	Speak, Salisbury – at least, if thou canst, speak.
	How far'st thou, mirror of all martial men?
	One of thy eyes and thy cheek's side struck off!
5	Accursèd tower! Accursèd fatal hand
	That hath contrived this woeful tragedy!
	In thirteen battles Salisbury o'ercame;
	Henry the Fifth he first trained to the wars;
	Whilst any trump did sound or drum struck up
10	His sword did ne'er leave striking in the field.
	Yet liv'st thou, Salisbury? Though thy speech doth fail,
	One eye thou hast to look to heaven for grace;
	The sun with one eye vieweth all the world.
	Heaven, be thou gracious to none alive,
15	If Salisbury wants mercy at thy hands!
	Thou shalt not die whiles –
	He beckons with his hand, and smiles on me,
	As who should say, 'When I am dead and gone,
	Remember to avenge me on the French.'
20	Plantagenet, I will — and like thee, Nero,
	Play on the lute, beholding the towns burn.
	Wretched shall France be only in my name.
	Here an alarum, and it thunders and lightens
	What stir is this? What tumult's in the heavens?
24	Whence cometh this alarum and the noise?

Henry VI, part 1

The General

The General is the commander of the French garrison at Bordeaux during in the latter years of 'The Hundred Years War' between England and France. The English commander, Talbot, has just arrived at the walls of the city and demanded its surrender. This is the General's response.

He doesn't appear anywhere else in the play and he could be any age above mid-twenties.

---

1   *owl* (Regarded as a bird of ill omen often foretelling death.)
3   *period* end
4   *but by death* only through your own death
7 & 25 *Dauphin* heir to the French throne (This is 'Dolphin' in some editions.)
      appointed equipped
9   *either hand thee* both sides of you
      pitched drawn up in battle order
10   *wall thee* block you
11   *redress* help
12   *front* confront
      apparent spoil inevitable capture (and subsequent slaughter)
13   *pale* (i.e. the complexion of death.)
14   *ta'en the sacrament* (i.e. sworn an oath.)
15   *fire* (This is 'rive' in some editions.)
19   *latest* final
20   *due* courtesy
      withal with
21   *the glass that now begins to run* (i.e. the sand begins to 'run' in an hourglass – a proverbial way of saying that 'time is running out.')
22   *sandy hour* (i.e. the 'hour' that it takes the sand to 'run' through the hourglass.)
23   *well coloured* (i.e. healthy.)
25   *warning bell* (i.e. a bell for giving alarms or tolling for the dead.)
26   *heavy* sombre

Act 4, Scene 2
General –

1   Thou ominous and fearful owl of death,
       Our nation's terror and their bloody scourge,
       The period of thy tyranny approacheth.
       On us thou canst not enter but by death;
5   For, I protest, we are well fortified
       And strong enough to issue out and fight.
       If thou retire, the Dauphin well appointed
       Stands with the snares of war to tangle thee.
       On either hand thee there are squadrons pitched
10   To wall thee from the liberty of flight,
       And no way canst thou turn thee for redress
       But death doth front thee with apparent spoil,
       And pale destruction meets thee in the face.
       Ten thousand French have ta'en the sacrament
15   To fire their dangerous artillery
       Upon no Christian soul but English Talbot.
       Lo, there thou stand'st, a breathing valiant man
       Of an invincible unconquered spirit.
       This is the latest glory of thy praise,
20   That I thy enemy due thee withal,
       For ere the glass that now begins to run
       Finish the process of his sandy hour,
       These eyes that see thee now well colourèd
       Shall see thee withered, bloody, pale, and dead.
           Drum afar off
25   Hark, hark, the Dauphin's drum, a warning bell,
       Sings heavy music to thy timorous soul,
27   And mine shall ring thy dire departure out.   *Exit*

Henry VI, part 1

The Earl of Suffolk

The Earl (later Duke) of Suffolk (William de la Pole; 1396–1450) was a corrupt nobleman and an inept military leader and politician. However, Shakespeare departs significantly from the historical record in his dramatisation of Suffolk's relationship with Margaret (of Anjou). Immediately before this scene in the play, Joan of Arc (La Pucelle) has been captured by the English at the battle of Angiers – historically, this happened in the year that the real Margaret was born. Clearly here Margaret is a beautiful young woman and it seems safe to assume that Shakespeare thought of Suffolk being in his twenties at this point.

His only appearance prior to this is briefly to state his position in the faction fighting over who has the best claim to be king of England. Signs of his later deviousness don't appear until after this speech.

I have cut two lines of Margaret's to construct this speech.

---

3   *reverent* (This is 'reverend' in some editions.)

4–5 (These lines are reversed in some editions.)

4   *for* in mark of

9   *allotted* destined

10 & 11 *his* (This is 'her' in some editions; I prefer the male form to link the protective swan to Suffolk himself.)

12   *servile usage* treatment as a prisoner

16   *glassy* reflecting

17   *counterfeited beam* (i.e. reflecting back an image of the sun, thus giving the illusion of a second sun.)

21   *de la Pole* (Suffolk's family name.)
      disable not thyself! don't undervalue yourself!

22   *Is she not here to hear?* (There are several variations of this sentence: 'Is she not prisoner here?'; 'Is she not here?'; 'Is she not here thy prisoner?')

23   *a woman's sight* the sight of a woman

24–25 *such / Confounds* such that it confounds

25   *rough* unstable

Act 5, Scene 3 (Scene 5 in some editions)
Suffolk –

> *Alarum. Enter the Earl of Suffolk with Margaret in his hand*
1   Be what thou wilt, thou art my prisoner.
> *He gazes on her*
     O fairest beauty, do not fear nor fly,
     For I will touch thee but with reverent hands;
     I kiss these fingers for eternal peace,
5   And lay them gently on thy tender side.
     Who art thou, say, that I may honour thee?
     An earl I am, and Suffolk am I called.
     Be not offended, nature's miracle,
     Thou art allotted to be ta'en by me;
10   So doth the swan his downy cygnets save,
     Keeping them prisoner underneath his wings.
     Yet if this servile usage once offend,
     Go, and be free again, as Suffolk's friend.
> *She is going*
     O stay! [*Aside*] I have no power to let her pass.
15   My hand would free her, but my heart says no.
     As plays the sun upon the glassy stream,
     Twinkling another counterfeited beam,
     So seems this gorgeous beauty to mine eyes.
     Fain would I woo her, yet I dare not speak.
20   I'll call for pen and ink, and write my mind.
     Fie, de le Pole, disable not thyself!
     Hast not a tongue? Is she not here to hear?
     Wilt thou be daunted at a woman's sight?
     Ay, beauty's princely majesty is such
25   Confounds the tongue, and makes the senses rough.

Henry VI, part 2

The Duke of Suffolk

The Duke of Suffolk (William de la Pole; 1396–1450) was a corrupt nobleman and an inept military leader and politician. However, Shakespeare departs significantly from the historical record in his dramatisation of Suffolk's relationship with Margaret (of Anjou). Suffolk captured her at the battle of Angiers (in *Henry VI, part 1*) and instantly fell in love with her, but because he was already married he decided to offer her as a bride to the king and secretly make her his mistress – 'I will rule both her, the King, and realm.' In this play he sets about removing any opposition to his dreams of power – including arranging the murder of the popular Duke of Gloucester, a brother of the king. Suspicion immediately falls on Suffolk and the king is pressured into banishing him. At this point, he is left alone with Margaret who is suddenly unsympathetic, saying to him, 'Fie, coward woman and soft-hearted wretch! / Hast thou not spirit to curse thine enemy?' This speech is his response.

Historically, he was about fifty at the time, but Shakespeare appears to have thought of him as being around twenty years younger.

Margaret interrupts his final line, so it could be cut for audition.

----

2   *the mandrake's groan* (It was believed that this plant, with its forked root supposed to resemble the human body, shrieked when pulled out of the ground and caused the hearer to die or go mad.)
3   *searching* cutting
4   *curst* savage
5   *fixèd* gritted
9   *sparkle like the beaten flint* (When two pieces of flint are struck together sparks are produced.)
10   *on* (This is 'an' in some editions.)
     distract mad (This is 'distraught' in some editions.)
11   *ban* denounce
14   *Gall* (The bitter fluid secreted by the liver into the gall-bladder.)
     daintiest most delicious
15   *cypress trees* (These were associated with funerals, graveyards and death.)
16   *basilisks* (Mythical beasts the sight of which was said to be fatal and the name of the largest type of Elizabethan cannon.)
17   *smart* painful
18   *frightful* as terrifying
19   *boding* ominous
     screech-owls (Birds whose cries were thought to herald death.)
     make the consort full! complete the company of musicians!

Act 3, Scene 2
Suffolk –

1   A plague upon them! Wherefore should I curse them?
     Could curses kill, as doth the mandrake's groan,
     I would invent as bitter searching terms,
     As curst, as harsh, and horrible to hear,
5   Delivered strongly through my fixèd teeth,
     With full as many signs of deadly hate,
     As lean-faced Envy in her loathsome cave.
     My tongue should stumble in mine earnest words;
     Mine eyes should sparkle like the beaten flint;
10   My hair be fixed on end, as one distract;
     Ay, every joint should seem to curse and ban.
     And, even now, my burdened heart would break
     Should I not curse them. Poison be their drink!
     Gall, worse than gall, the daintiest that they taste!
15   Their sweetest shade, a grove of cypress trees!
     Their chiefest prospect, murd'ring basilisks!
     Their softest touch as smart as lizards' stings!
     Their music frightful as the serpent's hiss,
     And boding screech-owls make the consort full!
20   All the foul terrors in dark-seated hell –

Henry VIII

The Third Gentleman

The Third Gentleman is part of a small group of minor courtiers who describe and discuss major events of the play. Although they serve a similar function to Shakespeare's choric characters (in *Henry V*, for instance) they are far more open about their opinions of events. Sometimes these are at variance with the 'official line' and could land them in trouble if expressed more publicly. They seem to be well-informed about what's going on in 'high places' and keen to share facts and opinions with close colleagues but are without the power to influence events. Beyond this we know very little about any of their ages or backgrounds; although, from the references in this speech, this Gentleman could have had a naval background and he seems (from dialogue at the end of this scene) to have slightly more influence and authority than his companions. In this speech he is describing the sumptuous coronation of Henry VIII's second wife, Anne Boleyn.

Historically, this event marks the triumphant (for some) end of a turbulent period in English politics. After twenty years of marriage, Henry, desperate for a male heir and with an eye for Anne, had instituted divorce proceedings against his first wife, Katherine of Aragon, who had only produced one surviving daughter. These 'proceedings' stretched out over about five years and severely strained relations with the powerful Catholic Church.

I have changed the first sentence of the speech to make it self-contained. An alternative might be, 'Sir, I will speak it to you.'

----

3   *fell off* withdrew
6   *opposing* exhibiting
8   *goodliest* fairest
11 *the shrouds* (the ropes that are part of) a ship's rigging
13 *Doublets* Tight-fitting jackets
16 *rams* battering-rams
17 *press* crowd
20 *in one piece* like a piece of cloth

Act 4, Scene 1
Third Gentleman –

1   Sir, let me speak it to you. The rich stream
Of lords and ladies, having brought the Queen
To a prepared place in the choir, fell off
A distance from her; while her grace sat down
5   To rest a while – some half an hour or so –
In a rich chair of state, opposing freely
The beauty of her person to the people.
Believe me, sir, she is the goodliest woman
That ever lay by man; which when the people
10   Had the full view of, such a noise arose
As the shrouds make at sea in a stiff tempest,
As loud and to as many tunes. Hats, cloaks –
Doublets, I think – flew up, and had their faces
Been loose, this day they had been lost. Such joy
15   I never saw before. Great-bellied women,
That had not half a week to go, like rams
In the old time of war, would shake the press,
And make 'em reel before 'em. No man living
Could say 'This is my wife' there, all were woven
20   So strangely in one piece.

Henry VIII

Griffith

Griffith is a gentleman usher to Queen Katherine first wife of Henry VIII. She only had one surviving child (Mary) and after twenty years of marriage, Henry, desperate for a male heir and with an eye for Anne Boleyn, wanted to divorce her – a very difficult task under the rules of the Roman Catholic Church. The divorce proceedings began in 1528 with Cardinal Wolsey (the King's closest advisor) pleading Henry's case. Katherine violently objected to the Cardinal, calling him, 'my most malicious foe, and think not / At all a friend to truth.' Eventually the divorce was granted and she lived the rest of her life in comfortable surroundings in the country provided for her by Henry. Not long after the divorce Wolsey himself lost the King's favour and died.

In the play Griffith is attendant upon his mistress throughout the divorce proceedings, but does very little beyond pass on messages. In this scene, he has just arrived to bring Katherine the news of Wolsey's death. She proceeds to speak of his corrupt practices; Griffith tries to redress the balance with this speech – aware that she is not far from death herself.

Although he is mentioned in the historical record, we know nothing about him. He could be any age above about thirty.

I have cut two short lines of Katherine's to create this speech.

---

2   *live in brass* (i.e. are fixed in people's memories.)
4   *speak his good* describe his good qualities
6   *from an humble stock* (Wolsey was the son of a merchant; it was then very unusual for one of this kind of background to rise so very high in the establishment.)
11 *sought him* (i.e. 'sought his friendship'.)
12 *were unsatisfied in getting* was never satisfied that all the riches he acquired were sufficient
15 *raised* built (Wolsey founded colleges at Ipswich, his birthplace, and at Oxford; the latter still exists as Christ Church.)
      in you in your name
16 *One of which fell with him* (i.e. Ipswich.)
17 *did* inspired
18 *The other* (i.e. the one in Oxford.)
19 *art* learning
      rising (i.e. in fame and in structure.)
22 *felt* knew

Act 4, Scene 2
Griffith –

1   Noble madam,
        Men's evil manners live in brass; their virtues
        We write in water. May it please your highness
        To hear me speak his good now?
5   This Cardinal,
        Though from an humble stock, undoubtedly
        Was fashioned to much honour. From his cradle
        He was a scholar, and a ripe and good one;
        Exceeding wise, fair-spoken, and persuading;
10   Lofty and sour to them that loved him not,
        But to those men that sought him, sweet as summer.
        And though he were unsatisfied in getting –
        Which was a sin – yet in bestowing, madam,
        He was most princely: ever witness for him
15   Those twins of learning that he raised in you,
        Ipswich and Oxford! One of which fell with him,
        Unwilling to outlive the good that did it;
        The other, though unfinished, yet so famous,
        So excellent in art, and still so rising,
20   That Christendom shall ever speak his virtue.
        His overthrow heaped happiness upon him;
        For then, and not till then, he felt himself,
        And found the blessèdness of being little.
        And to add greater honours to his age
25   Than man could give him, he died fearing God.

King John

Cardinal Pandulph

Cardinal Pandulph (sometimes 'Pandulf'; d. 1226) is a Papal Legate. Prior to his arrival, a dispute between King John and King Philip (of France) looks as though it has been settled and the two kings are to be united through the marriage of Philip's son, Lewis, and John's niece, Blanche. Pandulph interrupts the wedding celebrations with a demand from the Pope that King John give way in a dispute over the archbishopric of Canterbury. John will not give way so Pandulph excommunicates him and demands that Philip break the new alliance and make war on John. Philip eventually agrees, encouraged by his son, Lewis. The English win the first battle and capture John's nephew, Prince Arthur, who had been sheltered by Philip and whose right to the English throne was at the root of the initial dispute between the two kings.

After the battle Pandulph tries to encourage Philip and Lewis when they are interrupted by Arthur's despairing mother, Constance. When she leaves ('tearing her hair') Philip follows her fearing 'some outrage'. Pandulph takes this opportunity to give Lewis more encouragement and suggest a plan to turn their fortunes: John will probably kill Arthur and thus alienate his own followers, and Lewis (through his marriage to Blanche) will have a legitimate claim to the English throne on Arthur's death. Lewis is still pessimistic, so Pandulph comes out with this speech.

Pandulph is a highly accomplished diplomat who can twist almost any argument his own way. He could be any age over about thirty.

---

2   *lays you plots* makes plans which could benefit you
      the times conspire with you the circumstances seem favourable for your purposes
3   *steeps* risks (literally, soaks)
      true royal (i.e. that of Arthur, the rightful heir.)
4   *bloody safety and untrue* insecurity and guilt
5   *This act* (i.e. John's murder of Arthur.)
      vilely (This is 'evilly' in some editions.)
      born conceived (This is 'borne' in some editions.)
6   *zeal* (i.e. in John's cause.)
7   *none so small advantage* no opportunity, however small
8   *check his reign* interfere with his government
9   *exhalation* meteor
10   *No scope of nature* Nothing within the scope of nature
      distempered stormy
11   *customèd* ordinary
12   *pluck away his natural cause* disregard its natural explanation
13   *meteors* (These were believed supernatural heavenly signs, as opposed to the 'natural exhalation' of line 9.)
      prodigies and signs portents and indications of the future
14   *Abortives* Untimely births (seen as fore-telling future calamities)
      presages, tongues of heaven omens (of disaster), signs indicating the will of heaven
15   *denouncing* proclaiming

Act 3, Scene 4 (Scene 3 in some editions)
Pandulph –

1   How green you are, and fresh in this old world!
         John lays you plots; the times conspire with you;
         For he that steeps his safety in true blood
         Shall find but bloody safety and untrue.
5   This act, so vilely born, shall cool the hearts
         Of all his people, and freeze up their zeal,
         That none so small advantage shall step forth
         To check his reign but they will cherish it.
         No natural exhalation in the sky,
10   No scope of nature, no distempered day,
         No common wind, no customèd event,
         But they will pluck away his natural cause,
         And call them meteors, prodigies and signs,
         Abortives, presages, and tongues of heaven
15   Plainly denouncing vengeance upon John.

King John

Hubert de Burgh

Hubert de Burgh (d. 1243) was one of the highest-ranking aristocrats in England, however Shakespeare departs significantly from the historical record giving him a lower status. To add further confusion, in some editions he first appears as a representative of the city of Angiers (an English occupied city in France) who brokers a settlement between King John and King Philip II of France. The dispute between the two kings is over John's right to the English throne: the latter's deceased elder brother, Geoffrey, had a son (Arthur) whom Philip maintains is the rightful king.

Hubert next appears after the truce has broken down; the two sides fight and Arthur (previously protected by Phillip) is captured by John, who hands him over to Hubert for safe-keeping. Then John secretly asks Hubert to kill Arthur. At the last minute the jailer cannot carry out his master's request, but he tells John that he has carried out the task. Not long afterwards Hubert suddenly appears before John and comes out with this speech, hoping that his master will regret Arthur's supposed death and that then the truth can be revealed.

He is usually played middle-aged, but could be twenty years younger.

I have cut a short line of King John's to construct this speech.

1–3 *five moons... in wondrous motion.* (Such astronomical irregularities were commonly regarded as portents of calamity.)
2 *fifth* (This is 'fith' in some editions.)
4 *beldams* old women (This is 'beldames' in some editions.)
5 *prophesy upon it dangerously* (1) predict calamity from these signs; (2) interpret these signs in a way which is dangerous (to the kingdom)
9 *grip* (This is 'gripe' in some editions.)
10 *action* gestures
14 *swallowing* taking in eagerly
16 *on* in
   slippers (Tailors generally worked barefoot.)
18 *a many thousand* many thousands of
19 *embattailèd and ranked* drawn up in well-ordered positions ready for battle
   Kent (i.e. only about twenty miles from the shore of France.)
20 *artificer* workman
21 *Cuts off his tale* Interrupts his story

Act 4, Scene 2
Hubert –

> *Enter Hubert*
>
> 1   My lord, they say five moons were seen tonight –
>   Four fixèd, and the fifth did whirl about
>   The other four in wondrous motion.
>   Old men and beldams in the streets
> 5   Do prophesy upon it dangerously.
>   Young Arthur's death is common in their mouths,
>   And when they talk of him they shake their heads,
>   And whisper one another in the ear;
>   And he that speaks doth grip the hearer's wrist,
> 10 Whilst he that hears makes fearful action,
>   With wrinkled brows, with nods, with rolling eyes.
>   I saw a smith stand with his hammer, thus,
>   The whilst his iron did on the anvil cool,
>   With open mouth swallowing a tailor's news,
> 15 Who, with his shears and measure in his hand,
>   Standing on slippers which his nimble haste
>   Had falsely thrust upon contrary feet,
>   Told of a many thousand warlike French
>   That were embattailèd and ranked in Kent.
> 20 Another lean unwashed artificer
> 21 Cuts off his tale, and talks of Arthur's death.

King Lear

The Earl of Kent

The Earl of Kent is a nobleman loyal to King Lear, but when the king disinherits his youngest daughter, Cordelia, Kent is the first to protest and Lear banishes him from the kingdom. Kent then disguises himself and becomes a servant to Lear. When Oswald (steward to Goneril, one of the king's two elder daughters) fails to treat the king with due respect, Kent trips him up and shoves him away. A few scenes later they encounter each other again. Oswald is condescending and says to the still-disguised Kent, 'I know thee not.' This is Kent's response edited together from several speeches.

To enhance his disguise, Kent says that he will 'other accents borrow'. He also tells Lear that 'I have years on my back forty-eight.' Although he is generally played around this age, I don't see why he couldn't be played (undisguised) ten, even twenty years younger – especially given his vigour against Oswald.

Different editions have a stage direction, 'He draws his sword', at various places between 'yet the moon shines.' (line 13) and 'cullionly barber-monger, draw!' (line 14) – you have to decide where suits you best.

1–2 *broken meats* discarded scraps of food (with the sense of them being only fit for animals)
2 *three-suited* (i.e. only having three suits, which was servant's annual allowance.)
3 *hundred-pound* (i.e. buying the status of a gentleman without have the background of one.)
   worsted-stocking wearer of woollen stockings (gentlemen wore silk)
4 *action-taking* (i.e. taking legal action instead of fighting.)
   glass-gazing vain (through admiring himself in the mirror too much)
4–5 *super-serviceable* always ready to serve (his master; with the implication that he'd even go as far as a dishonourable or dishonest action)
5 *finical* finicky
   one-trunk-inheriting possessing no more than will fit into a single trunk
6 *be a bawd in way of good service* go as far as procuring prostitutes as part of his duties
7 *composition* combination
9–10 *thy addition* the titles I have given you
13 *make a sop o' th' moonshine of you* pierce your body so much that it can soak up moon-light (like a biscuit dunked in a cup of tea)
14 *cullionly* rascally
   barber-monger frequent visitor to barber's shops (i.e. a fop.)
16 *Vanity the puppet* (i.e. Goneril.)
17 *carbonado your shanks* slash your legs (like meat being prepared for cooking)
18 *come your ways!* come on!
19 *neat slave* foppish rascal

Act 2, Scene 2 (Scene 7 in the Quarto edition)
Kent –

1   Fellow, I know thee for a knave, a rascal, an eater of broken
     meats; a base, proud, shallow, beggarly, three-suited,
     hundred-pound, filthy worsted-stocking knave; a lily-
     livered, action-taking, whoreson, glass-gazing, super-
5   serviceable, finical rogue; one-trunk-inheriting slave; one that
     wouldst be a bawd in way of good service, and art nothing
     but the composition of a knave, beggar, coward, pander, and
     the son and heir of a mongrel bitch; one whom I will beat into
     clamorous whining if thou deniest the least syllable of thy
10   addition. What a brazen-faced varlet art thou, to deny thou
     knowest me! Is it two days since I tripped up thy heels and
     beat thee before the King? Draw, you rogue; for though it be
     night, yet the moon shines. I'll make a sop o' th' moonshine
     of you, you whoreson, cullionly barber-monger, draw! Draw,
15   you rascal. You come with letters against the King, and take
     Vanity the puppet's part against the royalty of her father.
     Draw, you rogue, or I'll so carbonado your shanks – draw,
     you rascal, come your ways! Strike, you slave! Stand, rogue!
19   Stand, you neat slave! Strike!

Love's Labour's Lost

Berowne

Berowne (or Biron) is one of the three young lords attending the King of Navarre. At the beginning of the play the latter, determined that court shall become a centre for scholarship, requires that they all sign an oath dedicating themselves to academic study for the next three years and to forswear other pleasures, including the company of women. To help enforce this abstinence the King has decreed 'that no woman shall come within a mile of my court.' Berowne points out that the Princess of France is about to arrive on a diplomatic mission and cannot be ignored. The compromise is to meet outside the court where Berowne and Rosaline exchange sharp witticisms – inside the cynical Berowne is smitten with her, as are his companions with other ladies. Shortly afterwards he secretly writes to her and just before this speech employs Costard (a clown) to deliver the letter. Costard has just left and Berowne is alone.

---

1   *And I forsooth in love! I, that have been love's whip* (This line is divided into two separate ones and/or prefaced with the exclamation 'O!' in some editions.)

2   *beadle* (minor parish officer whose duties included the whipping of petty offenders.)
    humorous love-sick

4   *pedant* schoolmaster (with the sense of one who puts much stress on detail and formal rules)

4 & 6 *boy* (i.e. Cupid, the Roman god of love who legend said was a beautiful young boy and fired his arrows of love (and sexual desire) whilst blindfold.)

5   *Than whom no mortal so magnificent!* Compared with whom no mortal is so arrogant!

6   *wimpled* blindfolded   *purblind* completely blind

7   *Signor Junior* (Cupid may be only a boy, but he has immense power.)
    Dan Sir ('Dan' is a variant of 'Don', a contraction of Latin 'Dominus')

8   *Regent* Ruler   *folded arms* (i.e. a sign of disappointment in love.)

11   *plackets, codpieces* (The former were petticoats (or the slits therein); the latter were bagged appendages worn by men over their breeches in the genital area. The sense here is in what lies underneath both.)

12   *imperator* absolute ruler

13   *paritors* (Officers of the church courts who summoned offenders, often for sexual offences.)

14   *corporal of his field* senior assistant (to Cupid) in this battle

15   *colours like a tumbler's hoop!* regimental ensignia so ostentatiously! (This was a hoop decorated with many-coloured ribbons.)

17   *German clock* (These were so elaborate, often including automatic figures of persons or animals, that they were often unreliable.)

18   *Still a-repairing, ever out of frame* Constantly in need of repair, always out of order

20   *being... right!* only working (or behaving) properly if constantly supervised!

21   *perjured* (i.e. by breaking the oath sworn at the beginning of the play.)

22   *among three* (i.e. amongst the three lords attending the King.)

23   *whitely* sallow

25   *do the deed* make love

26   *Argus* (A mythical monster with a hundred eyes, never all closed simultaneously.)

27   *watch* stay awake all night

28   *Go to!* Take care!

32   *Joan* (i.e. a peasant girl.)

Act 3, Scene 1
Berowne –

1   And I, forsooth, in love! I that have been love's whip,
    A very beadle to a humorous sigh,
    A critic, nay, a night-watch constable,
    A domineering pedant o'er the boy,
5   Than whom no mortal so magnificent!
    This wimpled, whining, purblind, wayward boy,
    This Signor Junior, giant dwarf, Dan Cupid,
    Regent of love-rhymes, lord of folded arms,
    Th' anointed sovereign of sighs and groans,
10   Liege of all loiterers and malcontents,
    Dread prince of plackets, king of codpieces,
    Sole imperator and great general
    Of trotting paritors – O my little heart!
    And I to be a corporal of his field,
15   And wear his colours like a tumbler's hoop!
    What? I love, I sue, I seek a wife? –
    A woman, that is like a German clock,
    Still a-repairing, ever out of frame,
    And never going aright, being a watch,
20   But being watched that it may still go right!
    Nay, to be perjured, which is worst of all;
    And among three to love the worst of all –
    A whitely wanton with a velvet brow,
    With two pitch-balls stuck in her face for eyes;
25   Ay, and, by heaven, one that will do the deed
    Though Argus were her eunuch and her guard.
    And I to sigh for her, to watch for her,
    To pray for her! Go to! It is a plague
    That Cupid will impose for my neglect
30   Of his almighty dreadful little might.
    Well, I will love, write, sigh, pray, sue, and groan.
32   Some men must love my lady, and some Joan.   *Exit*

Love's Labour's Lost

Holofernes

Holofernes is a pedantic schoolmaster, who loves nothing better than to prove his intellectual superiority through his use of language. He revels in gently correcting his constant companion the curate, Sir Nathaniel, and is mocked by some of the other characters. Although he may appear pompous and completely self-obsessed, he is very knowledgeable and later in the play shows his vulnerability.

At this point he, Sir Nathaniel and Dull (the constable) have been conversing when they are approached by Jaquenetta (a country wench). She asks the curate to read out a letter she has received as she cannot read herself. Sir Nathaniel does so and then Holofernes can't help but take over the situation.

He is usually played middle-aged, but could be younger.

I have cut a response that Jaquenetta gives (after 'was this directed to you?') in order to construct this speech.

----

1   *find not the apostrophus* ignore the apostrophes ('apostrophas' in some editions)
    accent (correct) emphasis
2   *supervise the canzonet* look over the short poem (or song)
    Sir Nathaniel, (This is not in some editions.)
3   *only numbers ratified* merely metrically correct verses
    elegancy, facility elegance, fluency
4   *cadence* rhythmical flow
    caret it is lacking
4 & 5 *Ovidius Naso* (A famous Roman poet, whose family name was 'Naso' which means 'big-nose'.)
6   *jerks of invention* flashes of imagination
    Imitari To imitate (Latin)
7   *tired* attired (with saddle, reins, and other trappings)
8   *domicella* maiden (This is 'damosella' in some editions.)
9   *overglance the superscript* look over the greeting (at the beginning of the letter)
11   *intellect* contents and meaning
    nomination of the party name of the person
12–13 *in all desired employment* in any service you may desire of me
13   *Berowne* (This is 'Biron' in some editions.)
14   *votaries* (i.e. bound to by a vow.)
15   *sequent* follower
    Queen's (He means the Princess'.)
16   *by the way of progression* en route (passing from hand to hand)
17   *Trip and go* (from a popular dance-song)
18   *concern much* be of great importance
18–19 *Stay not thy compliment; I forgive thy duty.* Don't waste time on a polite farewell; I excuse you from curtseying (her 'duty').

Act 4, Scene 2
Holofernes –

1   You find not the apostrophus, and so miss the accent. Let me
supervise the canzonet. [*He takes the letter*] Sir Nathaniel, here
are only numbers ratified; but for the elegancy, facility, and
golden cadence of poesy, *caret*. Ovidius Naso was the man.

5   And why indeed 'Naso' but for smelling out the odoriferous
flowers of fancy, the jerks of invention? *Imitari* is nothing. So
doth the hound his master, the ape his keeper, the tired horse
his rider. But, *domicella* – virgin – was this directed to you? I
will overglance the superscript: 'To the snow-white hand of

10   the most beauteous Lady Rosaline.' I will look again on the
intellect of the letter for the nomination of the party writing
to the person written unto: 'Your ladyship's in all desired
employment, Berowne.' Sir Nathaniel, this Berowne is one of
the votaries with the King, and here he hath framed a letter

15   to a sequent of the stranger Queen's, which, accidentally or
by the way of progression, hath miscarried. [*To Jaquenetta*]
Trip and go, my sweet, deliver this paper into the royal hand
of the King; it may concern much. Stay not thy compliment; I

19   forgive thy duty. Adieu.

Love's Labour's Lost

Holofernes

Holofernes is a pedantic schoolmaster, who loves nothing better than to prove his intellectual superiority through his use of language. He revels in gently correcting his constant companion the curate, Sir Nathaniel, and is mocked by some of the other characters. Although he may appear pompous and completely self-obsessed, he is very knowledgeable and later in the play shows his vulnerability.

At this point Sir Nathaniel has just mentioned a conversation he had with 'a companion of the King's, who is entitled, nominated, or called Don Adriano de Armado.' – Holofernes cannot resist commenting with this speech.

He is usually played middle-aged, but could be younger.

I have cut a line of Sir Nathaniel's to create this speech.

---

1   *Novi hominem tanquam te* I know the man as well as I know you. (This is classroom Latin.)
     humour disposition

2   *peremptory* imperious
     his tongue filed his language polished and refined

2–3 *his gait majestical* his way of moving is stately

4   *thrasonical* boastful
     picked fastidious
     spruce over-elaborate

5   *odd* peculiar
     peregrinate affectedly foreign

6–7 *finer than the staple of his argument* thinner than the fibre of his subject-matter

7   *phantasimes* beings full of fantasies

8   *insociable* impossible to associate with
     point-device affectedly precise (This is 'point-devise' in some editions.)

8–9 *rackers of orthography* tormentors of spelling (Some Elizabethan educators believed that the pronunciation of English words should follow their spelling.)

9   *sine 'b'* without the 'b' ('sine' is 'fine' in some editions.)

11 *clepeth* calls
     calf, half (Holofernes would sound the 'l's in these words.)

12 *vocatur* is called

13 *abhominable* (This is how 'abominable' was spelled in Shakespeare's time; Holofernes would sound the 'h'.)

13–14 *It insinuateth me of insanire* It subtly drives one mad (Or as he says 'make frantic, lunatic.'; 'insanire' is 'insanie' in some editions.)

14 *ne intelligis, domine?* do you understand, sir?

Act 5, Scene 1
Holofernes –

1 *Novi hominem tanquam te.* His humour is lofty, his discourse
   peremptory, his tongue filed, his eye ambitious, his gait
   majestical, and his general behaviour vain, ridiculous, and
   thrasonical. He is too picked, too spruce, too affected, too
5 odd, as it were, too peregrinate, as I may call it. He draweth
   out the thread of his verbosity finer than the staple of his
   argument. I abhor such fanatical phantasimes, such
   insociable and point-device companions, such rackers of
   orthography as to speak 'dout', *sine* 'b', when he should say
10 'doubt'; 'det' when he should pronounce 'debt' – 'd, e, b, t',
   not 'd, e, t'. He clepeth a calf 'cauf', half 'hauf', neighbour
   vocatur 'nebour' – 'neigh' abbreviated 'ne'. This is
   abhominable – which he would call 'abominable'. It
   insinuateth me of *insanire – ne intelligis, domine?* – to make
15 frantic, lunatic.

Love's Labour's Lost

Berowne

Berowne (or Biron) is one of the three young lords attending the King of Navarre. The Princess of France and three of her ladies arrive on a diplomatic mission and the young men are each secretly smitten with the arrivals. Eventually, the men discover that the others all feel the same and plan to hold an entertainment where they can woo their particular ladies. Beforehand, they each send gifts of jewellery and poems and plan to approach the ladies disguised as a delegation of Russians. The ladies learn of this and decide to be masked and wear each other's jewellery. The men are completely taken in: each professing their love to the wrong lady. Then the ladies remove their masks and the men retreat in disarray. After a short while they return (without their Russian disguises) and the ladies mock them by talking about the 'fools' dressed as Russians whom they'd met earlier. Very quickly the men realise that they've been found out and Rosaline (Berowne's fancy) says to him, 'Why look you so pale? / Sea-sick, I think, coming from Muscovy.' This is his response.

---

1   *pour the stars down plagues* (Certain diseases were believed to be sent the planets.)
     for perjury for our (attempted) deception
2   *face of brass hold longer out?* brazen-faced affrontery hold out any longer?
4   *confound* destroy
     flout scorn
6   *keen conceit* sharp wit
7   *wish* entreat
8   *wait* attend upon you
11   *visor* disguise
     friend sweetheart
12   *blind harper's song* (Playing the harp or fiddle was a common way for the blind to earn their living.)
14   *Three-piled* The richest (The best quality velvet had a deep pile.)
     spruce over-elaborate
     affectation (This is 'affection' in some editions.)
15   *Figures* Turns of phrase
16   *blown* filled
     maggot ostentation nauseous showing off
20   *russet* simple (This was the colour of peasants' clothes.)
     kersey simple (Kersey was coarse woollen cloth.)
21   *wench* (In Shakespeare's time this was a term of affection.)
     law! indeed!
22   *sans* without

Act 5, Scene 2
Berowne –

1   Thus pour the stars down plagues for perjury.
       Can any face of brass hold longer out?
       Here stand I, lady; dart thy skill at me –
       Bruise me with scorn, confound me with a flout,
5   Thrust thy sharp wit quite through my ignorance,
       Cut me to pieces with thy keen conceit;
       And I will wish thee never more to dance,
       Nor nevermore in Russian habit wait.
       O, never will I trust to speeches penned,
10   Nor to the motion of a schoolboy's tongue,
       Nor never come in visor to my friend,
       Nor woo in rhyme, like a blind harper's song.
       Taffeta phrases, silken terms precise,
       Three-piled hyperboles, spruce affectation,
15   Figures pedantical – these summer flies
       Have blown me full of maggot ostentation.
       I do forswear them, and I here protest,
       By this white glove – how white the hand, God knows –
       Henceforth my wooing mind shall be expressed
20   In russet yeas and honest kersey noes.
       And to begin, wench, so God help me, law!
22   My love to thee is sound, sans crack or flaw.

Macbeth

The Bleeding Sergeant

The Bleeding Sergeant (some editions refer to him as a 'Captain') is a soldier in the armies of King Duncan (of Scotland) who repel those of 'The merciless Macdonwald' and the Norwegian invaders. He only appears in this scene and we learn nothing more about him beyond Malcolm's (son of King Duncan) introduction of him, 'This is the sergeant, / Who like a good and hardy soldier fought / 'Gainst my captivity.' Malcolm goes on to ask the Sergeant for 'knowledge of the broil' and this is his response.

He could be almost any age you like.

There are some variations in lineation between editions. I have cut Duncan's lines and adapted one of the Sergeant's to create this speech.

---

3   *choke their art* make impossible to swim (through 'clinging together')
     Macdonwald (This is 'Macdonald' in some editions.)
4   *to that* as if to that purpose
5–6 *The multiplying villainies of nature* Hosts of rebels (like insects and other creatures that irritate and sting)
6   *Western Isles* Hebrides (Islands north-west of Scotland.)
7   *Of* With
     kerns and gallowglasses light- and heavy-armed foot soldiers
8   *quarrel* cause (This is 'quarry' in some editions.)
9   *Showed* Appeared
10   *that name* (i.e. the title, 'brave')
13   *minion* beloved favourite
14   *the slave* (i.e. Macdonwald.)
15   *Which ne'er shook hands nor bade farewell to him* (i.e. killed him instantly allowing no time for human courtesies.)
16   *nave to th' chops* navel to the jaw
18   *'gins his reflection* begins its turning back (at the vernal equinox)
19   *break* (This word is not in some editions.)
20   *spring* source
21   *swells* wells up
23   *skipping* (Because they are lightly armed, they can run and weave about over the rough terrain very quickly.)
24   *Norweyan* (This is 'Norwegian' in some editions.)
     surveying vantage seeing his opportunity
25   *furbished* cleaned-up
28   *cracks* charges
     so in such a way
30   *Except* Unless
31   *memorize another Golgotha* make the battlefield as memorable for slaughter as Golgotha (i.e. the hill of Calvary, 'the place of skulls', where Christ was crucified.)

Act 1, Scene 2
Bleeding Sergeant –

1   Doubtful it stood,
    As two spent swimmers that do cling together
    And choke their art. The merciless Macdonwald –
    Worthy to be a rebel, for to that
5   The multiplying villainies of nature
    Do swarm upon him – from the Western Isles
    Of kerns and gallowglasses is supplied,
    And fortune on his damnèd quarrel smiling
    Showed like a rebel's whore. But all's too weak,
10   For brave Macbeth – well he deserves that name –
    Disdaining fortune, with his brandished steel
    Which smoked with bloody execution,
    Like valour's minion carved out his passage
    Till he faced the slave –
15   Which ne'er shook hands nor bade farewell to him
    Till he unseamed him from the nave to th' chops,
    And fixed his head upon our battlements.
    As whence the sun 'gins his reflection
    Shipwrecking storms and direful thunders break,
20   So from that spring whence comfort seemed to come
    Discomfort swells. Mark, King of Scotland, mark.
    No sooner justice had, with valour armed,
    Compelled these skipping kerns to trust their heels
    But the Norweyan lord, surveying vantage,
25   With furbished arms and new supplies of men,
    Began a fresh assault.
    Dismayed not, Macbeth and Banquo were as
    Cannons overcharged with double cracks, so
    They doubly redoubled strokes upon the foe.
30   Except they meant to bathe in reeking wounds
    Or memorize another Golgotha,
    I cannot tell –
33   But I am faint. My gashes cry for help.

Macbeth

The Porter

The Porter only appears in this scene and, apart from the few words that I have cut, says no more than is here. His references to 'equivocators' relates to the trial of Father Garnet, who was executed in 1606 for his complicity in the Gunpowder Plot.

He is generally played middle-aged but could be younger.

I have cut a few lines of Macduff's and made some minor word changes to construct this speech.

---

2   *old* had more than enough of

3   *Beelzebub* (The Devil; this is 'Belzebub' in some editions.)

3–4 *Here's a farmer that hanged himself on th' expectation of plenty* (i.e. a farmer who hoarded grain, hoping that prices would rise, but when he realised that there was going to be a surplus (an 'expectation of plenty') and that prices would fall, he hanged himself.)

5   *Come in time!* You've come at a good time! (This 'Come in, time-pleaser' in some editions.) *enough* (This is 'enow' in some editions.)

7, 10 & 23 *equivocator* (i.e. someone who seems to be expressing one thing but means another.)

12   *stealing out of a French hose* (Customers would bring cloth to a tailor to have 'hose' (breeches) made. When the fashion was for loose-fitting hose it was easy for the tailor to steal some of the cloth; however, when the fashion changed to tight-fitting ('French') hose, it became more likely that any theft would be noticed.)

13   *roast your goose* (1) heat your smoothing iron ('goose'); (2) 'cook your goose' (do for yourself) (Possibly, he may be referring to 'killing the goose that laid the golden eggs', just as the tailor was caught out trying to get rich quickly.)

17–18 *I pray you remember the porter* (i.e. 'Don't forget to give me a tip.')
Macduff and Lennox (Scottish noblemen.)

19   *second cock* three o'clock in the morning (It is now not long after dawn.)

26–7 *equivocates him in a sleep* fulfils his lechery only in a dream (and therefore deceives him)

27   *giving him the lie* (1) deceives him; (2) lays him out; (3) makes him urinate ('lye' is slang for urine)

30   *took up my legs* made me fall over
made a shift managed

31   *cast him* (1) throw him off; (2) vomit

Act 2, Scene 3
Porter –

Enter a Porter. Knocking within

1 Here's a knocking indeed! If a man were porter of hell-gate
he should have old turning the key. [*Knock within*] Knock,
knock, knock. Who's there, i' th' name of Beelzebub? Here's
a farmer that hanged himself on th' expectation of plenty.

5 Come in time! Have napkins enough about you; here you'll
sweat for 't. [*Knock within*] Knock, knock. Who's there, in th'
other devil's name? Faith, here's an equivocator that could
swear in both the scales against either scale, who committed
treason enough for God's sake, yet could not equivocate to

10 heaven. O, come in, equivocator. [*Knock within*] Knock,
knock, knock. Who's there? 'Faith, here's an English tailor
come hither for stealing out of a French hose. Come in, tailor.
Here you may roast your goose. [*Knock within*] Knock, knock.
Never at quiet. What are you? – But this place is too cold for

15 hell. I'll devil-porter it no further. I had thought to have let in
some of all professions that go the primrose way to th'
everlasting bonfire. [*Knock within*] Anon, anon! I pray you
remember the porter. [*He opens the gate*]

Enter Macduff and Lennox

Faith, sir, we were carousing till the second cock, and drink,

20 sir, is a great provoker of three things: nose-painting, sleep,
and urine. Lechery, sir, it provokes and unprovokes: it
provokes the desire but it takes away the performance.
Therefore much drink may be said to be an equivocator with
lechery: it makes him and it mars him; it sets him on and it

25 takes him off; it persuades him and disheartens him, makes
him stand to and not stand to; in conclusion, equivocates him
in a sleep, and, giving him the lie, leaves him. And drink did
give me the lie last night, sir, i' the very throat on me; but I
requited him for his lie, and, I think, being too strong for him,

30 though he took up my legs sometime, yet I made a shift to

31 cast him.

Macbeth

Malcolm

Malcolm is the elder son of King Duncan of Scotland. At the beginning of the play the King's army has won a resounding victory over a rebel force. Duncan rewards the hero of the battle, Macbeth, with the title and estates of the defeated Thane of Cawdor. He also proclaims Malcolm as heir to the throne. After the murder of his father Malcolm (and his brother Donalbain) flee the country, fearing for their lives ('There's daggers in men's smiles') and that suspicion may fall on them. Macbeth becomes king and Malcolm seeks refuge in the English court, where he is joined (in this scene) by Macduff, a Scottish nobleman. Malcolm is suspicious of his visitor (not unreasonably, as Macbeth has agents everywhere) and in spite of Macduff's vehement affirmation that he is 'not treacherous' Malcolm still has his 'doubts'. For instance, Macduff has left his family ('Those precious motives, those strong knots of love') in Scotland, where they must be in danger if he is truly on Malcolm's side and against Macbeth. Macduff is about to leave when Malcolm comes out with this speech.

Historically, Malcolm did a lot of good for his country, and Shakespeare couldn't overtly make him seem to be worse than Macbeth as James I (King of England and Scotland when the play was first performed) would have taken exception. However, as I read the text, I believe that Shakespeare's Malcolm has the potential to be in 'All the particulars of vice so grafted'.

He is probably in his early-mid twenties.

This is three speeches edited together – you could simply go as far as 'With my confineless harms' (line 19).

---

2   *absolute fear* complete distrust
3   *think* realise that
5   *withal* besides
6   *hands uplifted* people to support
    right (i.e. as the legitimate King of Scotland.)
7   *gracious England* (i.e. Edward the Confessor, the English king.)
12 *and more* and in more
15 *particulars* varieties
    grafted ingrained
16 *opened* come out (i.e. like buds, as suggested by 'grafted')
19 *confineless* boundless
20 *Luxurious* Lecherous
21 *Sudden* Violent
25 *cistern* (This is 'cestern' in some editions.)
26 *continent* restraining

Act 4, scene 3
Malcolm –

1   Be not offended.
       I speak not as in absolute fear of you.
       I think our country sinks beneath the yoke.
       It weeps, it bleeds, and each new day a gash
5   Is added to her wounds. I think withal
       There would be hands uplifted in my right,
       And here from gracious England have I offer
       Of goodly thousands. But for all this,
       When I shall tread upon the tyrant's head,
10   Or wear it on my sword, yet my poor country
       Shall have more vices than it had before,
       More suffer, and more sundry ways, than ever,
       By him that shall succeed.
       It is myself I mean; in whom I know
15   All the particulars of vice so grafted
       That, when they shall be opened, black Macbeth
       Will seem as pure as snow, and the poor state
       Esteem him as a lamb, being compared
       With my confineless harms. Macbeth is bloody,
20   Luxurious, avaricious, false, deceitful,
       Sudden, malicious, smacking of every sin
       That has a name. But there's no bottom, none,
       In my voluptuousness. Your wives, your daughters,
       Your matrons, and your maids could not fill up
25   The cistern of my lust; and my desire
       All continent impediments would o'erbear
       That did oppose my will. Better Macbeth
28   Than such an one to reign.

Measure for Measure

Pompey Bum

Pompey Bum is a pimp and servant of Mistress Overdone, the brothel-keeper. Early in the play, a crackdown on prostitution is announced and he is brought to court for his activities. The first time this occurs, he manages to talk his way out of his situation, but is warned that he will be whipped if he is brought before the court again 'upon any complaint whatsoever.' Later he is caught with a 'strange picklock' (i.e. a skeleton key) and is immediately sent to prison, where he is offered parole if he will assist the executioner with beheadings planned for four o'clock the following day. He agrees and just before the appointed time he comments upon his fellow inmates with this speech.

He could be any age above about mid-twenties.

---

1   *am as well acquainted* have as many acquaintances
1–2 *house of profession* (i.e. the brothel for which he works.)
4   *Rash* (i.e. implying that he's reckless.)
     in for a commodity (Money-lenders, in order to obtain more than the lawful interest of ten per cent, would force borrowers to take commodities, at a value determined by the lender, to sell on as part of their loans – here, 'brown paper and old ginger', which had a much greater value in Shakespeare's time compared to nowadays.)
5–6 *nine score and seventeen pounds, of which he made five marks ready money* (i.e. The money-lender has valued the 'brown paper and old ginger' at £197 and Rash only managed to sell it for just over £3 (a mark was two-thirds of a pound).)
7   *for* (This is 'or' in some editions.)
     old women (were traditionally fond of ginger.)
8   *Caper* (i.e. implying that he likes frolicking about.)
9   *Threepile the mercer* (i.e. implying that he's a dealer ('mercer') in high-quality, deep-pile cloth.)
10 *peaches him* accuses him (of being)
11 *Dizzy* (i.e. implying that he's foolish.) (This is 'Dizie' or 'Dizy' in some editions.)
     Deepvow (i.e. implying that he's a prolific swearer.)
12 *Copperspur* (i.e. implying that he's worthless because it wasn't gold.)
     Starve-lackey (i.e. implying that he's an underfed servant.)
13 *Drop-heir* (i.e. implying that he's father of illegitimate children; this is 'Drop-hair' in some editions.)
     lusty Pudding (i.e. implying that he's hearty eater of sausage = 'pudding'.)
14 *Forthright the tilter* (i.e. implying that he's straightforward – as a 'tilter' would ride his horse straight forward in a tilt or joust.)
     brave showily dressed
     Shoe-tie (i.e. implying that he's got elaborate decorations on his shoes which were a foreign importation, hence 'the great traveller'.)
15 *wild Half-can that stabbed pots* (i.e. implying that he's a tapster who falsified the capacity marks on ale-pots to his advantage.) ('Pots' has a upper-case 'P' in some editions which changes the sense.)
16 *doers in our trade* (i.e. users of our brothel.)
16–17 *'for the Lord's sake'*. (i.e. prisoners, who beg from the gratings of their cells with this cry.)

Act 4, Scene 3
Pompey –

Enter Pompey

1   I am as well acquainted here as I was in our house of profession. One would think it were Mistress Overdone's own house, for here be many of her old customers. First, here's young Master Rash; he's in for a commodity of brown

5   paper and old ginger, nine score and seventeen pounds, of which he made five marks ready money. Marry, then ginger was not much in request, for the old women were all dead. Then is there here one Master Caper, at the suit of Master Threepile the mercer, for some four suits of peach-coloured

10   satin, which now peaches him a beggar. Then have we here young Dizzy, and young Master Deepvow, and Master Copperspur and Master Starve-lackey the rapier and dagger man, and young Drop-heir that killed lusty Pudding, and Master Forthright the tilter, and brave Master Shoe-tie the

15   great traveller, and wild Half-can that stabbed pots, and I think forty more, all great doers in our trade, and are now 'for

17   the Lord's sake'.

Much Ado About Nothing

Leonato

Leonato is governor of Messina and father of Hero. Until this scene he appears a warm, kindly man; fond of a joke but aware of the responsibilities of his office.

The play opens with the return, from victories in war, of Don Pedro (Prince of Aragon) and other lords including a young courtier, Claudio, who is highly praised for having 'borne himself beyond the promise of his age'. Very soon he and Hero fall in love and Leonato readily agrees to their marriage. However, Claudio (and Don Pedro) are persuaded through a malicious trick that Hero has been 'disloyal'. Claudio is enraged and at the altar rejects Hero: 'this rotten orange' who 'knows the heat of a luxurious bed'. Hero denies the accusations, but Claudio (backed by Don Pedro) insists that they are true – Hero faints and they storm out of the church. The remaining wedding party think that she might be dead, but then she stirs and Leonato says, 'Dost thou look up?'; the Friar comments, 'Yea, wherefore should she not?' and Leonato erupts into this speech.

Interestingly, no mother for Hero is mentioned throughout the play, so we can presume that he has been in sole charge of her upbringing for a number of years – creating a special bond between them.

He is generally played middle-aged but could be as young as thirty.

---

1   *Wherefore?* (This is 'Wherefore!' in some editions.)
3   *printed in her blood* undoubtedly true (and shown by her blushes)
6   *shames* feelings of shame
7   *on the rearward of reproaches* immediately after reproaching you
8   *but one* (i.e. only one child.)
9   *Chid I* Did I ask to be rebuked ('Chid')
       that at frugal nature's frame? a 'frugal' scheme that gave me only one child?
10   *one too much by thee* you are one too many
14   *smirchèd* thus stained so
17 & 18 *mine* (i.e. my daughter.)
19   *was to myself not mine* had no thought for my self
20   *Valuing of her* Because I valued her so exclusively
21   *that* so that
23–24 *season give / To* restore (Salt was used as a preservative.)

Act 4, Scene 1
Leonato –

1   Wherefore? Why, doth not every earthly thing
        Cry shame upon her? Could she here deny
        The story that is printed in her blood?
        Do not live, Hero, do not ope thine eyes;
5   For did I think thou wouldst not quickly die,
        Thought I thy spirits were stronger than thy shames,
        Myself would on the rearward of reproaches
        Strike at thy life. Grieved I, I had but one?
        Chid I for that at frugal nature's frame?
10   O one too much by thee! Why had I one?
        Why ever wast thou lovely in my eyes?
        Why had I not with charitable hand
        Took up a beggar's issue at my gates,
        Who smirchèd thus and mired with infamy,
15   I might have said 'No part of it is mine,
        This shame derives itself from unknown loins.'
        But mine, and mine I loved, and mine I praised,
        And mine that I was proud on, mine so much
        That I myself was to myself not mine,
20   Valuing of her – why she, O she is fallen
        Into a pit of ink, that the wide sea
        Hath drops too few to wash her clean again,
        And salt too little which may season give
24   To her foul tainted flesh.

Richard II

Thomas Mowbray

Thomas Mowbray, Duke of Norfolk (c. 1365–1400) was one of the highest ranking nobles of the time. In 1384 he was given the title of Earl Marshal of England by Richard II and helped to arrange his master's marriage to Isabel of France in 1396.

At the beginning of the play King Richard summons his first cousin Henry Bolingbroke, Duke of Hereford (and later King Henry IV), to make public ('face to face') his (as yet unspecified) accusations against Mowbray. The two men appear before the king and he asks Bolingbroke, 'what dost thou object / Against the Duke of Norfolk, Thomas Mowbray?' After claiming that his only concern is for the king's 'precious safety', he accuses Mowbray of being 'a traitor and a miscreant' without giving specific details. This is Mowbray's response.

Later in the play it transpires that Mowbray is guilty of at least one of Bolingbroke's charges – murdering the Duke of Gloucester – but that he had acted on the king's direct orders.

Historically, he was in his early thirties at the time, but he could be played younger.

---

1   *Let not my cold words here accuse my zeal* Don't let my calm language cast doubt upon my loyalty ('cold words' implies a deep underlying anger and shock.)

2   *a woman's war* (i.e. fought with words alone.)

3   *eager* sharp

4   *Can* That can

5   *cooled* (i.e. through death.)

10   *else* otherwise

     post hasten (Literally, to travel using relays of horses and hence very fast for that time.)

11   *These terms of treason* (i.e. 'traitor and miscreant')

13   *let him be* assuming that he were

17   *tied* obliged

     afoot on foot

19   *inhabitable* not inhabitable

21   *this* (i.e. the statement in the next line and / or his sword on which he lays his hand.)

Act 1, Scene 1
Mowbray –

1   Let not my cold words here accuse my zeal.
    'Tis not the trial of a woman's war,
    The bitter clamour of two eager tongues,
    Can arbitrate this cause betwixt us twain.
5   The blood is hot that must be cooled for this.
    Yet can I not of such tame patience boast
    As to be hushed and naught at all to say.
    First, the fair reverence of your highness curbs me
    From giving reins and spurs to my free speech,
10   Which else would post until it had returned
    These terms of treason doubled down his throat.
    Setting aside his high blood's royalty,
    And let him be no kinsman to my liege,
    I do defy him, and I spit at him,
15   Call him a slanderous coward and a villain;
    Which to maintain I would allow him odds,
    And meet him, were I tied to run afoot
    Even to the frozen ridges of the Alps,
    Or any other ground inhabitable,
20   Wherever Englishman durst set his foot.
    Meantime let this defend my loyalty –
22   By all my hopes, most falsely doth he lie.

Romeo and Juliet

Benvolio

Benvolio is a close friend and cousin of Romeo and the two appear together several times in the early part of the play. With Romeo behaving in a lovesick fashion, Benvolio and Mercutio (also a Montague and a mutual friend) tease him but Benvolio calls a halt when he feels that Mercutio is going too far. In this scene Benvolio and Mercutio encounter a group from the rival family, the Capulets, led by the hot-headed Tybalt (Juliet's cousin). Both Mercutio and Tybalt are spoiling for a fight, but Benvolio tries to calm things down. Then Romeo appears. Tybalt accuses the new arrival of being a 'villain', but he will not rise to the bait; Mercutio challenges Tybalt and Romeo tries to stop them fighting, but Mercutio is fatally wounded and Tybalt flees. Benvolio helps to carry Mercutio off to get help, but soon returns to report their friend's death to Romeo. Then Tybalt returns; Romeo suddenly flares up; they fight and Tybalt is killed. Benvolio tells his friend to flee whilst he stays to face the consequences. The Prince, together with members of both Romeo's and Tybalt's families, suddenly arrives and he interrogates Benvolio who responds with this speech.

He doesn't appear again in the play after this scene.

He could be any age between about mid-teens and mid twenties.

---

3   *nice* trivial

    withal as well

6   *take truce with the unruly spleen* come to terms with the uncalled for bad-temper

9   *all as hot* just as angry

10–11 *one hand... and with the other* (i.e. Mercutio and Tybalt fought with rapiers in their right hands and daggers in their left.)

13 *Retorts it* Parries it

15 *agile* (This is 'agent' in some editions.)

17 *envious* malicious

18 *stout* brave

20 *but newly entertained* only just contemplated the idea of

Act 3, Scene 1
Benvolio –

1   Tybalt, here slain, whom Romeo's hand did slay.
     Romeo, that spoke him fair, bid him bethink
     How nice the quarrel was, and urged withal
     Your high displeasure. All this – utterèd
5   With gentle breath, calm look, knees humbly bowed –
     Could not take truce with the unruly spleen
     Of Tybalt deaf to peace, but that he tilts
     With piercing steel at bold Mercutio's breast;
     Who, all as hot, turns deadly point to point,
10   And, with a martial scorn, with one hand beats
     Cold death aside, and with the other sends
     It back to Tybalt, whose dexterity
     Retorts it. Romeo, he cries aloud,
     'Hold, friends! Friends, part!' and swifter than his tongue
15   His agile arm beats down their fatal points,
     And 'twixt them rushes; underneath whose arm
     An envious thrust from Tybalt hit the life
     Of stout Mercutio, and then Tybalt fled;
     But by and by comes back to Romeo,
20   Who had but newly entertained revenge,
     And to 't they go like lightning. For ere I
     Could draw to part them was stout Tybalt slain,
     And as he fell did Romeo turn and fly.
24   This is the truth, or let Benvolio die.

Romeo and Juliet

Capulet

Capulet is a wealthy citizen of Verona, the head of his family and Juliet's father. In the early parts of the play he appears to be a strong, reasonable man and a kind father. Unusually for the time, he even insists that Paris, a wealthy suitor for his daughter's hand, must win 'her heart' before he'll give consent to their marriage. After the death in a street fight of Tybalt (his wife's nephew and Juliet's cousin), he suddenly changes his mind and decides that his daughter shall marry Paris on 'Thursday'. His wife tells Juliet (by now secretly in love with Romeo) of the plan; then Capulet (accompanied by Juliet's Nurse) appears. As soon as he hears of Juliet's refusal, he loses his temper. The Nurse tries to intervene on Juliet's behalf and then his wife says that he is 'too hot' (becoming too angry). This speech is his response.

He is usually played middle-aged, but Juliet is fourteen and his wife hints that she is only twenty-eight – so, he could be around thirty.

---

1   *God's bread!* (An oath. The bread is that consecrated in the Communion Service.)
(This line is split into two in some editions, with the second reading 'Day, night; hour, tide, time; work, play')

5   *demesnes* estates
nobly lined well born ('lined' is 'liened' or, even 'trained' in some editions.)

6   *parts* personal qualities

8   *puling* whimpering

9   *mammet* doll (This is 'maumet' in some editions.)
in her fortune's tender when she is offered a good chance (of marriage)

12   *an* if (This is 'and' in some editions.)

12   *I'll pardon you!* (i.e. in a negative sense.)

14   *I do not use to jest* I am not accustomed to joking

15   *Advise* Consider this seriously

16 & 17 *An If*

21   *I'll not be forsworn* I shall not change my mind (and break my promises)

Act 3, Scene 5
Capulet –

1   God's bread, it makes me mad! Day, night; work, play;
     Alone, in company, still my care hath been
     To have her matched; and having now provided
     A gentleman of noble parentage,
5   Of fair demesnes, youthful, and nobly lined,
     Stuffed, as they say, with honourable parts,
     Proportioned as one's thought would wish a man –
     And then to have a wretched puling fool,
     A whining mammet, in her fortune's tender,
10   To answer 'I'll not wed, I cannot love;
     I am too young, I pray you pardon me'!
     But an you will not wed, I'll pardon you!
     Graze where you will, you shall not house with me.
     Look to 't, think on 't. I do not use to jest.
15   Thursday is near. Lay hand on heart. Advise.
     An you be mine, I'll give you to my friend.
     An you be not, hang, beg, starve, die in the streets,
     For, by my soul, I'll ne'er acknowledge thee,
     Nor what is mine shall never do thee good.
20   Trust to 't. Bethink you. I'll not be forsworn.   *Exit*

The Taming of the Shrew

The Lord

The Lord only appears in the 'Induction' (i.e. Introduction or Prologue) to the play, which is often cut in production. We learn very little about him beyond the fact that he has quite a few servants and that a group of travelling players take the chance of calling on him, so he must be a well off country gentleman.

Very early in the play, he returns from hunting to find a tinker, Christopher Sly, in a drunken sleep. This speech is his reaction to the unconscious man.

I have cut the huntsmen's lines and two of the Lord's lines to construct this speech.

He could be any age you care.

---

2   *image* appearance (In his drunken state, Sly looks like a dead man.)
3   *practise* play a trick
5   *sweet* perfumed (Which was necessary as the technology to clean clothes properly did not exist at the time.)
7   *brave* elegantly dressed
8   *forget himself?* forget his own identity?
11 *Balm* Bathe
    distillèd waters (i.e. sweet-scented liquids, such as rose-water.)
14 *dulcet* pleasing
15 *straight* immediately
16 *reverence* bow
20 *ewer* (i.e. a jug with a wide spout, used to bring water for washing the hands.)
    diaper towel
25 *his disease* (i.e. implying that he's going mad.)
29 *kindly* (Also, implying 'convincingly'.)
30 *passing* extremely
31 *husbanded with modesty* managed with restraint

Induction, Scene 1
Lord –

1   O monstrous beast! How like a swine he lies.
       Grim death, how foul and loathsome is thine image.
       Sirs, I will practise on this drunken man.
       What think you: if he were conveyed to bed,
5   Wrapped in sweet clothes, rings put upon his fingers,
       A most delicious banquet by his bed,
       And brave attendants near him when he wakes –
       Would not the beggar then forget himself?
       Carry him gently to my fairest chamber,
10   And hang it round with all my wanton pictures.
       Balm his foul head in warm distillèd waters,
       And burn sweet wood to make the lodging sweet.
       Procure me music ready when he wakes,
       To make a dulcet and a heavenly sound.
15   And if he chance to speak, be ready straight,
       And with a low submissive reverence
       Say 'What is it your honour will command?'
       Let one attend him with a silver basin
       Full of rose-water and bestrewed with flowers;
20   Another bear the ewer, the third a diaper,
       And say 'Will 't please your lordship cool your hands?'
       Someone be ready with a costly suit,
       And ask him what apparel he will wear.
       Another tell him of his hounds and horse,
25   And that his lady mourns at his disease.
       Persuade him that he hath been lunatic,
       And when he says he is, say that he dreams,
       For he is nothing but a mighty lord.
       This do, and do it kindly, gentle sirs.
30   It will be pastime passing excellent,
31   If it be husbanded with modesty.

The Taming of the Shrew

Tranio

Tranio is a servant to Lucentio, a young gentleman of Pisa, and the two have just arrived in Padua where Lucentio plans serious study at the world-famous university. Initially, Lucentio extols the virtues of his plans – then, realising that he doesn't quite know what he's letting himself in for, he asks the servant for his opinion. This is Tranio's response.

Tranio is cleverer and more quick-witted than his master, and as the play progresses manages to carry through some outrageous subterfuges. He is probably in his early twenties, but could be older.

----

1   *Mi perdonate* Pardon me (Italian)
2   *in all affected as* in complete agreement with
7   *stoics* (Stoics believe in the repression of emotions in order to enhance the intellectual rigour of their studies.)
    stocks stupid, unfeeling people
8   *devote* devoted
    Aristotle (Ancient Greek philosopher who wrote on most areas of learning – including acting. He was famous for the rigorous logic he required in order to reach any conclusion.)
    checks cautions
9   *As* So that
    Ovid (A Roman poet, famous for his love poems.)
    abjured renounced
10 *Balk* Quibble over finer points of
    acquaintance acquaintances
11 *practise rhetoric* use self-consciously elaborate language
    common talk ordinary conversation
12 *poesy* poetry
    quicken stimulate
14 *Fall to them as you find your stomach serves you* Partake of them when you feel the inclination
15 *profit grows* progress is made (as a creative thinker)
    ta'en taken
16 *affect* enjoy

Act 1, Scene 1
Tranio –

1   *Mi perdonate*, gentle master mine.
       I am in all affected as yourself,
       Glad that you thus continue your resolve
       To suck the sweets of sweet philosophy.
5   Only, good master, while we do admire
       This virtue and this moral discipline,
       Let's be no stoics nor no stocks, I pray,
       Or so devote to Aristotle's checks
       As Ovid be an outcast quite abjured.
10   Balk logic with acquaintance that you have,
       And practise rhetoric in your common talk.
       Music and poesy use to quicken you;
       The mathematics and the metaphysics,
       Fall to them as you find your stomach serves you.
15   No profit grows where is no pleasure ta'en.
16   In brief, sir, study what you most affect.

The Taming of the Shrew

Hortensio

Hortensio is a young suitor to Bianca, the younger sister of Katherina, the 'shrew' of the play's title. Their father, Baptista, insists that Katherina must marry before her sister. Hortensio encourages Petruchio to woo Katherina by telling him that she is rich. Meanwhile, Hortensio disguises himself as a music teacher to Bianca, but is sent to teach her sister instead.

Hortensio has just entered and tells Baptista what has occurred in Katherina's music lesson with this speech.

I have adapted two lines of Baptista's and changed a few words in order to create this speech.

---

3   *hold with her* survive in her hands
4   *break her to it* train her to play it (Much as a horse is 'broken' to the bit.)
5   *broke the lute to me.* (i.e. broken the lute by hitting him over the head with it.)
6   *frets* (i.e. the fingering bars on a lute.)
7   *bowed* bent
9   *'Frets, call you these?' quoth she, 'I'll fume with them.'* (i.e. as in 'fret and fume'.)
11   *pate* head
       made way went through
13   *pillory* (A wooden frame with holes which held the head and hands of a criminal.)
15   *jack* (A term of contempt.)
       vile (This is 'vild' in some editions.)
16   *As had she studied* As if she had given a lot of careful thought

Act 2, Scene 1
Hortensio –

        Enter Hortensio with his head broke

1   I fear for your daughter and her music, sir.
        I think she'll sooner prove a soldier,
        Iron may hold with her, but never lutes.
        I cannot break her to it – 'twould be true
5   To tell that she hath broke the lute to me.
        I did but tell her she mistook her frets,
        And bowed her hand to teach her fingering,
        When, with a most impatient devilish spirit,
        'Frets, call you these?' quoth she, 'I'll fume with them.'
10   And with that word she struck me on the head,
        And through the instrument my pate made way,
        And there I stood amazèd for a while,
        As on a pillory, looking through the lute,
        While she did call me rascal fiddler,
15   And twangling jack, with twenty such vile terms,
16   As had she studied to misuse me so.

The Tempest

Stephano

Stephano is a butler who is drunk in all his appearances in the play. Some would argue that he has good reason to be, for the ship he was on has recently been wrecked in a storm and he managed to escape 'upon a butt of sack which the sailors heaved overboard' and was 'cast ashore' on an island. He hides his sack (a dry white wine) in a cave, makes himself a wooden bottle from 'the bark of a tree' and sets out to see if any of his companions are still alive. This is his first appearance in the play and, so far he doesn't seem to have encountered anybody (or anything) of any significance.

He is generally played middle aged but could be younger.

I have cut several of Caliban's interjections and a few of Stephano's words, and added a stage direction (before line 15) to create this speech.

---

3   *at a man's funeral* (i.e. his own, or his presumably drowned shipmates.)
5   *swabber* (A seaman whose job was to wash down the decks.)
15–16 *put tricks upon 's* delude us with tricks (as a conjuror or showman might do)
16 *savages* (This is 'salvages' in some editions.)
    men of Ind men of India (an extremely rare sight at that time)
18–19 *'As proper a man as ever went on four legs cannot make him give ground.'* (Probably his own version of the Riddle of the Sphinx: 'Which is the animal that has four feet in the morning, two at midday and three in the evening?' The answer is, 'Man, who in infancy crawls on all fours, who walks upright on two feet in maturity, and in his old age supports himself on a stick.')
20 *at'* at his
21 *ague* fever
22 & 26 *recover him* restore him (to health)
23 *Naples* (i.e. Stephano's home.)
24 *trod on neat's leather* wore good quality footwear ('neat's leather' is cow hide)
26 *take* ask
27 *that hath him* that buys him
28 *soundly* very well
28–29 *Here is that which will give language to you, cat* (He's referring to a proverb, 'Ale will make a cat talk.')
31 *chaps* jaws

Act 2, Scene 2
Stephano –

Enter Stephano, singing, with a wooden bottle in his hand

1   I shall no more to sea, to sea,
       Here shall I die ashore –
This is a very scurvy tune to sing at a man's funeral. Well,
here's my comfort.
[*He drinks and then sings*]

5   The master, the swabber, the boatswain, and I,
       The gunner and his mate,
       Loved Mall, Meg, and Marian, and Margery,
       But none of us cared for Kate
       For she had a tongue with a tang,
10   Would cry to a sailor, 'Go hang!'
       She loved not the savour of tar nor of pitch,
       Yet a tailor might scratch her where'er she did itch.
       Then to sea, boys, and let her go hang!
This is a scurvy tune too. But here's my comfort.
[*He drinks*]
[*A strange four-limbed creature suddenly appears in his view*]

15   What's the matter? Have we devils here? Do you put tricks
upon 's with savages and men of Ind, ha? I have not 'scaped
drowning to be afeard now of your four legs. For it hath been
said, 'As proper a man as ever went on four legs cannot make
him give ground.' And it shall be said so again, while
20   Stephano breathes at' nostrils. This is some monster of the
isle with four legs, who hath got, as I take it, an ague. I will
give him some relief. If I can recover him, and keep him tame,
and get to Naples with him, he's a present for any emperor
that ever trod on neat's leather. He shall taste of my bottle. If
25   he have never drunk wine afore, it will go near to remove his
fit. If I can recover him, and keep him tame, I will not take too
much for him. He shall pay for him that hath him, and that
soundly. Come on your ways. Open your mouth. Here is that
which will give language to you, cat. Open your mouth. This
30   will shake your shaking, I can tell you, and that soundly. You
31   cannot tell who's your friend. Open your chaps.

The Tempest

Ferdinand

Ferdinand is the young son of King Alonso of Naples. Their ship is wrecked in a storm and Ferdinand is thrown ashore on a strange island, separated from his father and other companions. He is enticed by strange music into the presence of Prospero (the ruler of the island) and his daughter, Miranda. The attraction between them is instant but in spite of Miranda's protests, Prospero accuses him of being a spy, manacles him and forces him to move a large pile of logs. Whilst carrying out this task, Ferdinand reflects that Miranda's support for him 'makes my labours pleasures' – suddenly she appears and urges him to 'Work not so hard'; even offers to take over the work herself. Then he asks her name 'that I might set it in my prayers'. She tells him and this is his response.

I have constructed this speech from two separate ones and cut a few lines.

----

4   *best* the highest
6 & 7 *several* particular individual
9   *quarrel with* undermine
     owed owned
10   *put it to the foil* cancelled it (i.e. the 'grace') out
17   *kind event* a favourable response
18   *If hollowly* If I am insincere
     invert turn
19   *boded me* destined for me
     mischief bad luck
20   *what else* whatsoever else

Act 3, Scene 1
Ferdinand –

1   Admired Miranda!
        Indeed the top of admiration, worth
        What's dearest to the world. Full many a lady
        I have eyed with best regard; and many a time
5   Th' harmony of their tongues hath into bondage
        Brought my too diligent ear. For several virtues
        Have I liked several women; never any
        With so full soul but some defect in her
        Did quarrel with the noblest grace she owed
10   And put it to the foil. But you, O you,
        So perfect and so peerless, are created
        Of every creature's best. Hear my soul speak:
        The very instant that I saw you did
        My heart fly to your service; there resides
15   To make me slave to it. And for your sake
        Am I this patient log-man. Witness this,
        And crown what I profess with kind event,
        If I speak true! If hollowly, invert
        What best is boded me to mischief! I,
20   Beyond all limit of what else i' th' world,
        Do love, prize, honour you.

The Tempest

Ariel

Ariel is a sprite or fairy – invisible to all but the magician Prospero, who rules the island (the setting of the play) and controls everybody and everything on it. Ariel's chief job is to carry out Prospero's wishes. At the beginning of the play he (or 'she' or 'it') contrived the wreck of the ship containing Prospero's enemies (Alonso, Sebastian, Antonio and others) whilst making sure that no-one was physically harmed. He leads the scattered survivors various merry dances round the island and not long before this speech Prospero arranges (magically) for a banquet to appear to the hungry men. They are just starting to eat when Ariel suddenly appears to them.

Ariel obviously enjoys his work – indeed, Prospero is very aware that in having all this fun Ariel might go too far in the heat of the moment. Ariel's moods go up and down quite violently – a bit like a child's. Ariel, the magical being, has very human feelings.

This is quite a long speech – you could start from, 'You fools! I and my fellows' (line 8).

Ariel can be played by either a man or a woman.

---

harpy (A fierce, filthy and greedy monster; half woman and half bird.)

2   *That hath to instrument* That has for use (i.e. the power.)
    this lower world (i.e. the Earth.)

3   *never-surfeited* always hungry

7   *such-like valour* the irrational courage of madness

8   *Their proper selves* Themselves

12   *still-closing waters* (waters which continually flow together again immediately after they've divided)

13   *dowle* small feather

14   *like* also

15   *massy* heavy

18   *From Milan did supplant* (Prospero was Duke of Milan before being ousted by these 'three'.)

19   *requit it* avenged (what they did to Prospero and, his daughter, Miranda)

24   *Ling'ring perdition* Slow ruin

27-30   *whose wraths... clear life ensuing* to escape the just retribution of these powers, repentance and a blameless future life is the only remedy. Otherwise, in this lonely place, they will have their revenge.

29   *is nothing but* there is no alternative but

30   *clear* blameless

Act 3, Scene 3
Ariel –

Thunder and lightning. Ariel descends like a harpy, claps wings
upon the table, and, with a quaint device, the banquet vanishes

1   You are three men of sin, whom Destiny –
That hath to instrument this lower world
And what is in 't – the never-surfeited sea
Hath caused to belch up you; and on this island
5   Where man doth not inhabit, you 'mongst men
Being most unfit to live. I have made you mad,
And even with such-like valour men hang and drown
Their proper selves.   *[Alonso, Sebastian, and Antonio draw]*
        You fools! I and my fellows
Are ministers of Fate. The elements,
10   Of whom your swords are tempered may as well
Wound the loud winds, or with bemocked-at stabs
Kill the still-closing waters, as diminish
One dowle that's in my plume. My fellow ministers
Are like invulnerable. If you could hurt,
15   Your swords are now too massy for your strengths,
And will not be uplifted.
     [Alonso, Sebastian, and Antonio stand amazed]
        But remember,
For that's my business to you, that you three
From Milan did supplant good Prospero;
Exposed unto the sea, which hath requit it,
20   Him and his innocent child; for which foul deed,
The powers, delaying not forgetting, have
Incensed the seas and shores, yea, all the creatures,
Against your peace. Thee of thy son, Alonso,
They have bereft, and do pronounce by me
25   Ling'ring perdition – worse than any death
Can be at once – shall step by step attend
You and your ways; whose wraths to guard you from –
Which here, in this most desolate isle, else falls
Upon your heads – is nothing but heart's sorrow
30   And a clear life ensuing.   *Ascends and vanishes in thunder*

Troilus and Cressida

Thersites

Thersites abuses everyone he encounters, however the Greek commanders in the play (in varying degrees) enjoy his vicious and hateful cynicism. His job seems to be to entertain the soldiers bogged down in the endless and pointless siege of Troy. Achilles, one of the commanders, describes him as 'my digestion' and 'a privileged man' – in spite of being called a 'fool' by Thersites.

Earlier in the play he crudely but wittily insults one of the Greek commanders, Ajax, who is too slow-witted to respond in kind so he beats Thersites. He is rescued by two other commanders, Achilles and Patroclus, whom he also insults but they are amused and encourage him to turn his wit upon other commanders. At this point he is on his own.

He could be in his twenties or older.

----

2 *elephant Ajax* (Earlier, Ajax is described as being as 'slow as the elephant'.)
   carry it win the honours
4 *'Sfoot* by God's foot (a mild oath)
6 *execrations* expressions of loathing
   engineer military strategist (This is 'enginer' in some editions.)
8 *thunder-darter* (One of Jove's titles.)
9 *Olympus* (A mountain in Greece and legendary home of the gods.)
10 *Mercury* (The messenger god with a reputation for cunning.)
   serpentine wily
   caduceus (Mercury's staff, which had two serpents entwined about it and had magical powers.)
11 *them* (i.e. Ajax and Achilles.)
12 *short-armed ignorance* (i.e. ignorance such that almost everything is beyond its understanding.)
13 *in circumvention* by craft
14 *massy irons* massive swords (which they use instead of intelligence)
16 *the Neapolitan bone-ache* (i.e. syphilis, which was supposed to have originated in Naples.)
17 *depending on* hanging over
   placket petticoat (or the slit in one, but the sense is what lies beyond)
18 *Envy* (i.e. himself.)

Act 2, Scene 3
Thersites –

Enter Thersites

1   How now, Thersites! What, lost in the labyrinth of thy fury!
Shall the elephant Ajax carry it thus? He beats me, and I rail
at him. O worthy satisfaction! Would it were otherwise – that
I could beat him, whilst he railed at me. 'Sfoot, I'll learn to
5   conjure and raise devils, but I'll see some issue of my spiteful
execrations. Then there's Achilles – a rare engineer. If Troy be
not taken till these two undermine it, the walls will stand till
they fall of themselves. O thou great thunder-darter of
Olympus, forget that thou art Jove, the king of gods, and,
10   Mercury, lose all the serpentine craft of thy caduceus, if ye
take not that little little, less than little wit from them that
they have – which short-armed ignorance itself knows is so
abundant scarce, it will not in circumvention deliver a fly
from a spider without drawing their massy irons and cutting
15   the web. After this, the vengeance on the whole camp! – or,
rather, the Neapolitan bone-ache, for that methinks is the
curse depending on those that war for a placket. I have said
my prayers, and devil Envy say 'Amen'. What ho! My Lord
19   Achilles!

Troilus and Cressida

Troilus

Troilus is the son of King Priam of Troy during the pointless and interminable siege of that city by the Greeks. He is insanely in love with Cressida, daughter of Chalchas, himself a deserter to the Greeks. Her uncle, Pandarus (now effectively her guardian) knows of Troilus' feelings for her and, earlier in the play, baits the young man mercilessly about his infatuation. However, Pandarus later agrees to arrange for the two to meet. Before he leaves to fetch her, he says provocatively to Troilus, 'Have you seen my cousin (i.e. Cressida)?' This is Troilus' response.

I have edited two speeches together and incorporated a slightly changed line of Pandarus'.

2–3 *Stygian banks... be thou my Charon.* (Dying was very often associated with reaching orgasm in Shakespeare's time.)

2 *Stygian banks* Banks of the Styx (In Greek mythology, this was the river that the souls of the dead were ferried across to reach Hades.)

3 *Staying for waftage* Waiting to be ferried
Charon (The ferryman – in Greek mythology.)

4 *fields* (i.e. the Elysian fields, where the souls of the good were transported after death.)

5 *wallow* (i.e. sexually.)
lily-beds (Also symbolic of sex.)

6 *Proposed for* Promised to

7 *painted* coloured

13 *wat'ry* salivating (in anticipation)
palate tastes (This is 'palates taste' in some editions.)

14 *repurèd* purified

15 *Swooning destruction* (This is 'Sounding destruction' in some editions.)

16 *subtle* (This is 'subtile' in some editions.)

19 *distinction in my joys* the capacity to discriminate between my 'joys'

20 *a battle* an army
on heaps en masse

Act 3, Scene 2
Troilus –

1   No, Pandarus, I stalk about her door
    Like a strange soul upon the Stygian banks
    Staying for waftage. O, be thou my Charon,
    And give me swift transportation to those fields
5   Where I may wallow in the lily-beds
    Proposed for the deserver! O gentle Pandar,
    From Cupid's shoulder pluck his painted wings
    And fly with me to Cressid.
    I'll walk i' th' orchard – you bring her straight.

                            Exit Pandarus

10   I am giddy; expectation whirls me round.
    Th' imaginary relish is so sweet
    That it enchants my sense. What will it be
    When that the wat'ry palate tastes indeed
    Love's thrice-repurèd nectar? Death, I fear me,
15   Swooning destruction, or some joy too fine,
    Too subtle-potent, tuned too sharp in sweetness,
    For the capacity of my ruder powers.
    I fear it much, and I do fear besides
    That I shall lose distinction in my joys,
20   As doth a battle when they charge on heaps,
21   The enemy flying.

Troilus and Cressida

Hector

Hector is the eldest son of King Priam of Troy, brother of Troilus and the city's leading warrior. He has a great enthusiasm for battle and the codes of chivalry. He is also capable of great sanity in the midst of the pointless and interminable siege of Troy by the Greek army. He points out the evil consequences of permitting 'the hot passion of distempered blood' to influence 'a free determination / 'Twixt right and wrong', however he tends to subsume such wisdom with his passion for personal honour and glory.

Early in the play he sends a challenge to the Greeks daring one of their number to fight him in hand-to-hand combat the following day – Ajax is selected.

In this scene, the combat is started but is soon stopped by others. Ajax expresses his keenness to continue, 'I am not warm yet', but Hector refuses with this speech.

He is probably in his twenties but could be older.

---

3   *cousin-german* first cousin
     emulation rivalry
6   *commixtion* mixed descent (This is 'commixion' in some editions.)
     so ordered in such a way
8   *Trojan* (This is 'Troyan' in some editions.)
10 *dexter* right
     sinister left
11 *multipotent* all-powerful
13 *impressure* mark
     rank exaggerated
     gainsay forbid
18 *him that thunders* (i.e. 'Jove')
19 *thus* (i.e. in an embrace of friendship.)

Act 4, Scene 5 (Scene 7 in some editions)
Hector –

1   Why then will I no more.
       Thou art, great lord, my father's sister's son,
       A cousin-german to great Priam's seed.
       The obligation of our blood forbids
5   A gory emulation 'twixt us twain.
       Were thy commixtion Greek and Trojan so
       That thou couldst say 'This hand is Grecian all,
       And this is Trojan; the sinews of this leg
       All Greek, and this all Troy; my mother's blood
10   Runs on the dexter cheek, and this sinister
       Bounds in my father's' – by Jove multipotent
       Thou shouldst not bear from me a Greekish member
       Wherein my sword had not impressure made
       Of our rank feud. But the just gods gainsay
15   That any drop thou borrowed'st from thy mother,
       My sacred aunt, should by my mortal sword
       Be drained. Let me embrace thee, Ajax.
       By him that thunders, thou hast lusty arms.
       Hector would have them fall upon him thus.
20   Cousin, all honour to thee.

Troilus and Cressida

Thersites

Thersites abuses everyone he encounters, however the Greek commanders in the play (in varying degrees) enjoy his vicious and hateful cynicism. His job seems to be to entertain the soldiers bogged down in the endless and pointless siege of Troy. Achilles, one of the commanders, describes him as 'my digestion' and 'a privileged man' – in spite of being called a 'fool' by Thersites. For his own part, he says of himself that he is 'lost in the labyrinth of (his own) fury' but 'I'll see some issue of my spiteful execrations'.

At this point he has been talking with Achilles and Patroclus (another Greek commander), who have just left him alone.

He could be in his twenties or older.

---

1   *blood* passion

1–3   *With... madmen* (Achilles and Patroclus may 'run mad' from excess of 'blood', but that they should go mad from excess of 'brain' is as likely as that Thersites should become a 'curer of madmen'.)

3   *Agamemnon* (The Greek Commander-in-Chief.)

4   *quails* (1) whores; (2) birds eaten as a delicacy (also thought to be amorous)

5–6   *transformation of Jupiter* (The god, Jupiter, transformed himself into a white bull to seduce Europa.)

6   *his brother, the bull* (Agamemnon's brother, Menelaus was the husband of Helen whose seduction and theft by Prince Paris of Troy was the spark that started the Trojan war. The bull's horns suggest the cuckold's horns.)
      primitive archetypal

7   *oblique* indirect (Since Jupiter did not cuckold anyone as Europa wasn't married.)
      thrifty worthy (He's being sarcastic.)
      shoeing-horn in a chain hanger-on

8–10   *to... to?* (i.e. Menelaus is so ludicrous that he is beyond satirical exaggeration.)

9   *forced* stuffed (This is 'farced' or 'faced' in some editions.)

10   *ass and ox* (i.e. fool and cuckold.)

12   *fitchew* polecat (supposed to be very libidinous, and notorious for its foul stench)
      puttock kite (a scavenging bird which feeds on carrion)

13   *herring without a roe* (and therefore useless)
      I would not care I wouldn't mind

13–14   *to be... destiny* (The threat of) being Menelaus would be enough to make me conspire against my fate

15   *care not to be* wouldn't object to being

16   *lazar* leper
      so provided that
      Hey-day! Hurrah!
      Sprites and fires! (The torches of the men approaching makes them appear like will o' the wisps or spirits.)

Act 5, Scene 1
Thersites –

1   With too much blood and too little brain these two may run
    mad; but if with too much brain and too little blood they do,
    I'll be a curer of madmen. Here's Agamemnon, an honest
    fellow enough, and one that loves quails, but he has not so
5   much brain as ear-wax. And the goodly transformation of
    Jupiter there, his brother, the bull, the primitive statue and
    oblique memorial of cuckolds, a thrifty shoeing-horn in a
    chain, hanging at his brother's leg – to what form but that he
    is, should wit larded with malice and malice forced with wit
10   turn him to? To an ass, were nothing; he is both ass and ox.
    To an ox, were nothing: he is both ox and ass. To be a dog, a
    mule, a cat, a fitchew, a toad, a lizard, an owl, a puttock, or a
    herring without a roe, I would not care; but to be Menelaus!
    – I would conspire against destiny. Ask me not what I would
15   be if I were not Thersites; for I care not to be the louse of a
16   lazar, so I were not Menelaus. Hey-day! Sprites and fires!

The Two Gentlemen of Verona

Proteus

Proteus is one of the 'Two Gentlemen'. Initially, he seems completely in love with Julia. His father, Antonio, decides that he must go to join his friend, Valentine (the other 'Gentleman'), in the court of the Duke of Milan to be 'tried and tutored in the world'. Proteus and Julia exchange rings and he vows to remain faithful whilst he is away. Meanwhile, Valentine has fallen in love with the Duke's daughter, Silvia, and they plan to elope. Proteus arrives, meets her and is immediately besotted himself. Valentine unaware of this complication asks Proteus to help in the elopement and then leaves to make his own preparations. Proteus, left on his own, confesses his new love and ponders whether he can 'check his love'. A short time later he builds on his earlier thoughts with this speech.

He could be anywhere between late teens and late twenties.

I have cut the final eleven lines to make this speech a better length for audition.

---

1 & 2 *shall I be forsworn* I will perjure myself (These two lines end with question marks in some editions – which changes the sense.)

4   *e'en* even

    that power (i.e. his love for Julia at the beginning of the play.)

7   *sweet-suggesting* seductive

11 *Unheedful* ill-considered

    heedfully with careful consideration

12 *wants* lacks

12 & 13 *wit* intelligence

12 *resolvèd* determined

    will intention

13 *learn* teach

14 *unreverent* irreverent (This is 'unreverend' in some editions.)

15 *preferred* urged

16 *soul-confirming* sworn on my soul

17 & 18 *leave to love* cease loving

18 *there* (i.e. Julia.)

23–4 *I... itself* (i.e. self-love is superior to love for a friend – very much against the code of friendship.)

24 *still* always

26 *swarthy Ethiope* (i.e. a black African – nowadays this would be considered racist, but in Shakespeare's time it was commonly used as the antithesis of the ideal of fair-skinned, English beauty.)

Act 2, Scene 6
Proteus –

Enter Proteus solus.

1   To leave my Julia, shall I be forsworn;
      To love fair Silvia, shall I be forsworn;
      To wrong my friend, I shall be much forsworn.
      And e'en that power which gave me first my oath
5   Provokes me to this threefold perjury.
      Love bade me swear, and love bids me forswear.
      O sweet-suggesting love, if thou hast sinned
      Teach me, thy tempted subject, to excuse it.
      At first I did adore a twinkling star,
10   But now I worship a celestial sun.
      Unheedful vows may heedfully be broken,
      And he wants wit that wants resolvèd will
      To learn his wit t' exchange the bad for better.
      Fie, fie, unreverent tongue, to call her bad
15   Whose sovereignty so oft thou hast preferred
      With twenty thousand soul-confirming oaths.
      I cannot leave to love, and yet I do;
      But there I leave to love where I should love.
      Julia I lose, and Valentine I lose;
20   If I keep them I needs must lose myself.
      If I lose them, thus find I by their loss:
      For Valentine, myself; for Julia, Silvia.
      I to myself am dearer than a friend,
      For love is still most precious in itself,
25   And Silvia – witness heaven that made her fair –
      Shows Julia but a swarthy Ethiope.
      I will forget that Julia is alive,
      Rememb'ring that my love to her is dead;
      And Valentine I'll hold an enemy,
30   Aiming at Silvia as a sweeter friend.
      I cannot now prove constant to myself
32   Without some treachery used to Valentine.

The Two Gentlemen of Verona

Valentine

Valentine is one of the 'Two Gentlemen'. At the beginning of the play, he is preparing to travel to the court of the Duke of Milan. He encourages his friend Proteus (the other 'Gentleman') to join him 'To see the wonders of the world abroad', but the latter is too much in love to leave home. Valentine teases him for this, but the two part promising to remain firm friends. In Milan, he finds himself falling in love with Silvia, the Duke's daughter, and they plan to elope as her father wants her to marry someone else. The Duke is informed of the details of the elopement and angrily banishes Valentine: 'Be gone, I will not hear thy vain excuse, / But as thou lov'st thy life, make speed from hence'. Left alone, Valentine muses on his desperate state with this speech.

He may seem like a somewhat gullible romantic leading man, but he is resourceful. Later he is prepared to tell lies in order to get out of a sticky situation, is quick to the rescue of Silvia when she is about to be raped and strongly threatens another rival suitor to her.

He could be anywhere between late teens and late twenties.

---

4   *deadly* deathlike
8   *shadow* illusion
13 *essence* very being
    leave cease
14 *influence* (This refers to the astrological 'influence' exerted by the star on human beings.)
16 *his* (i.e. (1) the Duke's or (2) 'death's'.)
    to fly in escaping
17 *attend on* wait for
18 *from life* (i.e. 'from' Sylvia.)

Act 3, Scene 1
Valentine –

1   And why not death, rather than living torment?
     To die is to be banished from myself,
     And Silvia is my self. Banished from her
     Is self from self – a deadly banishment.
5   What light is light, if Silvia be not seen?
     What joy is joy, if Silvia be not by –
     Unless it be to think that she is by,
     And feed upon the shadow of perfection.
     Except I be by Silvia in the night,
10   There is no music in the nightingale.
     Unless I look on Silvia in the day,
     There is no day for me to look upon.
     She is my essence, and I leave to be
     If I be not by her fair influence
15   Fostered, illumined, cherished, kept alive.
     I fly not death to fly his deadly doom:
     Tarry I here, I but attend on death;
18   But fly I hence, I fly away from life.

The Two Noble Kinsmen

Palamon

Palamon is one of the 'Noble Kinsmen'; the other is his cousin, Arcite. They are both young noblemen, nephews to the King of Thebes, Creon. In this scene, their first appearance, Arcite suggests leaving the corrupting influence that the city has become under their uncle's rule. In this speech, Palamon argues that they should stay and rise above that corruption.

Almost certainly this speech is Shakespeare's but because parts of the play were probably written by John Fletcher he is a somewhat confusing character. However, he is generally an honourable young man but given to interesting outbursts of belligerence and cynicism.

This is two speeches edited together and incorporating a short line of Arcite's.

---

2 *apes can tutor 's* we learn how to behave by those who misbehave (i.e. 'apes', who are also well-known mimics; 'tutor 's' = 'tutor us'.)

3 *What need* Why should

4 *Affect* Imitate (as an affectation)
   catching attractive

5 *Where there is faith?* When I believe in myself? (i.e. in the ways I conduct myself.)
   fond upon infatuated by

7 *conceived* understood
   saved (i.e. from punishment or damnation.)

8 *Speaking it truly?* If I speak what I believe to be the truth?

9 *generous bond to follow* obligation of honourable conduct to imitate

10–11 *Follows... pursuit* Who follows the advice of his tailor, perhaps for so long that eventually the tailor starts pursuing him (for an unpaid bill)

12 *unblest* out of favour

13 *for* because

14 *To such a favourite's glass?* To look like some fashionable trend-setter?
   canon rule

17 *street be foul* (It would appear highly affected to tip-toe through a clean street.)

19 *i' th' sequent trace* in the team (of 'horses') that follows (i.e. he doesn't want to follow, or imitate, anybody – he wants to lead.)

20 *plantain* (A herb used for treating superficial wounds.)

22 *unbounded* uncontrolled

24 *Beyond its power there's nothing* That there's no superior power to control it

25–26 *deifies alone / Voluble chance* makes men believe that inconstant Fortune has become the only god

26–28 *only attributes... act* claims that the achievements of others are due solely to his own skills

28-29 *commands men service, / And what they win in 't, boot and glory* demands men's service (in war) and also whatever profit ('boot') and glory they 'win'

30 *good, dares not* dare not do good

31 *sib* related (as in sibling)

32 *break* burst (from sucking too much blood)

Act 1, Scene 2
Palamon –

1   'Tis in our power –
Unless we fear that apes can tutor 's – to
Be masters of our manners. What need I
Affect another's gait, which is not catching
5   Where there is faith? Or to be fond upon
Another's way of speech, when by mine own
I may be reasonably conceived – saved, too,
Speaking it truly? Why am I bound
By any generous bond to follow him
10   Follows his tailor, haply so long until
The followed make pursuit? Or let me know
Why mine own barber is unblest – with him
My poor chin, too, for 'tis not scissored just
To such a favourite's glass? What canon is there
15   That does command my rapier from my hip
To dangle 't in my hand, or to go tiptoe
Before the street be foul? Either I am
The fore-horse in the team, or I am none
That draw i' th' sequent trace. These poor slight sores
20   Need not a plantain; that which rips my bosom
Almost to th' heart 's – our uncle Creon. He,
A most unbounded tyrant, whose successes
Makes heaven unfeared and villainy assured
Beyond its power there's nothing; almost puts
25   Faith in a fever, and deifies alone
Voluble chance; who only attributes
The faculties of other instruments
To his own nerves and act; commands men service,
And what they win in 't, boot and glory; one
30   That fears not to do harm, good, dares not. Let
The blood of mine that's sib to him be sucked
From me with leeches. Let them break and fall
33   Off me with that corruption.

The Two Noble Kinsmen

Arcite

Arcite is one of the 'Noble Kinsmen'; the other is his cousin, Palamon. They are both young noblemen, nephews to the villainous King of Thebes. Earlier in the play, the cousins decide that it is their duty to stay in the city and help fight the attack of Theseus (Duke of Athens) in spite of their misgivings about their uncle. In the ensuing war both are wounded and captured by Theseus. In prison, they reflect how much comfort they gain through being together and that their friendship will sustain them for the rest of their lives. Then, from their cell-window, they see Theseus' sister-in-law, Emilia (or 'Emily'), and both fall instantaneously in love with her. They quarrel over who has the best claim to her – deciding to fight a duel if ever there's an opportunity. Suddenly, Arcite is freed but banished (on pain of death) by Theseus. Arcite decides to take the risk of staying in order to woo Emilia and, disguised, enters a running and wrestling competition and wins. Impressed, Theseus invites Arcite to join his court as an attendant to Emilia. He next appears in this scene – the court is enjoying the May Day festivities in the woods near Athens – he is alone.

I have cut the opening three-and-a-half lines as they only serve to distract when this speech is performed in isolation from the play.

---

3   *buttons* buds
4   *enamelled knacks* brightly-coloured ornaments (i.e. flowers.)
     mead meadow
5   *bank of any nymph* (A river or stream personified by it's guardian spirit, a 'nymph' who had the form of a beautiful maiden.)
6   *makes the stream seem flowers* (i.e. the flowers on the banks are reflected on the surface of the water.)
7   *place* (This 'pace' in some editions.)
8   *rumination* deepest thinking
9   *eftsoons* soon
     come between enter into (your thoughts)
10   *chop on* take possession of
     cold chaste
11   *drop on* chance upon
11–12 *expectation / Most guiltless on 't* never expecting to
14   *takes strong note of me* observes me closely
15   *made me* allowed me to be
16   *prim'st* best
18   *backed* ridden
18-19 *field / That their crowns' titles tried* battlefield where their claims to the crown were decided
26   *eared* listened to
27   *passion* fit of anger
     enclose seize

Act 3, Scene 1
Arcite –

1   O Queen Emilia,
    Fresher than May, sweeter
    Than her gold buttons on the boughs, or all
    Th' enamelled knacks o' th' mead or garden – yea,
5   We challenge too the bank of any nymph
    That makes the stream seem flowers; thou, O jewel
    O' th' wood, o' th' world, hast likewise blessed a place
    With thy sole presence. In thy rumination
    That I, poor man, might eftsoons come between
10   And chop on some cold thought. Thrice blessèd chance
    To drop on such a mistress, expectation
    Most guiltless on 't. Tell me, O Lady Fortune,
    Next after Emily my sovereign, how far
    I may be proud. She takes strong note of me,
15   Hath made me near her, and this beauteous morn,
    The prim'st of all the year, presents me with
    A brace of horses – two such steeds might well
    Be by a pair of kings backed, in a field
    That their crowns' titles tried. Alas, alas,
20   Poor cousin Palamon, poor prisoner – thou
    So little dream'st upon my fortune that
    Thou think'st thyself the happier thing to be
    So near Emilia. Me thou deem'st at Thebes,
24   And therein wretched, although free. But if
    Thou knew'st my mistress breathed on me, and that
    I eared her language, lived in her eye – O coz,
27   What passion would enclose thee!

The Two Noble Kinsmen

Gerald

Gerald (or Geraldo) is a pedantic schoolmaster, who enjoys showing off his (self-perceived) command of language. He doesn't appear in any other scene, and is only briefly mentioned earlier as 'the dainty dominie' (fussy schoolmaster) in sole charge of organising an entertainment at the court of Duke Theseus. Earlier in this scene, he tries to instruct a group of 'villagers' on the dance they are to perform – amidst some chaos. Suddenly, there is the sound of hunting horns which signal the imminent arrival of the Duke's party; Gerald immediately sends the dancers off to await their cue. He then introduces the performance.

I have cut a line of the Duke's to construct this speech.

He is probably the creation of John Fletcher and not Shakespeare (the two playwrights are thought to have collaborated on this play), but very few people will worry about this for an audition.

---

4   *distinguish* describe as
5   *verity* truthfully   *fable* speak falsely
6   *rout* group
     rabble (This is 'rable' in some editions – which makes for a very clumsy rhyme with the previous line.)
7   *figure* (i.e. of speech.)
     chorus (This is 'choris' in some editions.)
8   *'fore* before
     morris Morris-dance (Commonly performed as part of the May festivities.)
9   *rectifier* corrector (or director)
10   *pedagogus* schoolmaster (Latin)
12   *ferula* cane
13   *machine, frame* (Pompous words for the 'structure' of the forthcoming entertainment.)
14   *dismal fame* reputation for creating dismay (in your enemies)
15   *Dis, Daedalus* (Dis was god of the underworld and Daedalus built the labyrinth in which the Minotaur was enclosed.)
16   *well-willer* well-wisher
18   *mickle* great
18-20 *'Morr'... 'Morris'* (He is probably holding up boards with the two syllables of the word, 'Morris'.)
21   *The body of our sport, of no small study* The chief item in our entertainment, prepared with great care
23   *tenor* summary (of what they are about to see. This is 'tenner' in some editions.)
24   *penner* pen-case (containing what I have 'penned'.)
25   *Lord of May and Lady bright* (The couple were chosen as Lord and Lady of May.)
27   *silent hanging* (i.e. a curtain which will safely conceal them if they hide behind it.)
29   *gallèd* travel-sore
30   *inflame the reck'ning* inflate the bill
31   *beest-eating Clown* ('Beest' is the very thick milk given by a cow immediately after the birth of a calf. It was considered dangerous, and therefore only a 'Clown' would drink it.)
32   *Babion* Baboon   *eke long tool* also a long penis
33   *Cum multis aliis* With many others (Latin)

Act 3, Scene 5
Gerald –

1   Thou doughty Duke, all hail! All hail, sweet ladies!
     If you but favour, our country pastime made is.
     We are a few of those collected here
     That ruder tongues distinguish 'villager';
5   And to say verity, and not to fable,
     We are a merry rout, or else a rabble,
     Or company, or, by a figure, *chorus*,
     That 'fore thy dignity will dance a morris.
     And I, that am the rectifier of all,
10   By title *pedagogus*, that let fall
     The birch upon the breeches of the small ones,
     And humble with a ferula the tall ones,
     Do here present this machine, or this frame;
     And, dainty Duke, whose doughty dismal fame
15   From Dis to Daedalus, from post to pillar,
     Is blown abroad, help me, thy poor well-willer,
     And with thy twinkling eyes, look right and straight
     Upon this mighty 'Morr' (of mickle weight) –
     'Is' now comes in, which being glued together
20   Makes 'Morris', and the cause that we came hither.
     The body of our sport, of no small study,
     I first appear, though rude, and raw, and muddy,
     To speak before thy noble grace this tenor,
     At whose great feet I offer up my penner.
25   The next, the Lord of May and Lady bright;
     The chambermaid and servingman, by night
     That seek out silent hanging. Then mine Host
     And his fat spouse, that welcomes to their cost
     The gallèd traveller, and with a beck'ning
30   Informs the tapster to inflame the reck'ning.
     Then the beest-eating Clown, and next the Fool,
     The Babion, with long tail and eke long tool,
     Cum multis aliis that make a dance;
34   Say 'Ay', and all shall presently advance.

The Two Noble Kinsmen

The Doctor

The Doctor only appears in two scenes and we learn very little about him beyond his obvious joy in the pomposity of his medical jargon. In this scene he has been brought to see the suddenly deranged daughter of the Jailer. First the Doctor observes the young woman, along with her father and a suitor for her hand (called the 'Wooer'). She rambles and sings confusedly with constant references to Palamon, a young nobleman. The Doctor diagnoses 'not an engrafted madness, but a most thick and profound melancholy' that he cannot 'minister to.' He asks if she 'affected any man ere she beheld Palamon'. Her father says that he 'was once, sir, in great hope she had fixed her liking on this gentleman, my friend.' The Wooer endorses this and the Doctor suddenly finds a remedy with this speech.

Some people believe that this speech (and some of the rest of the play) was written by Shakespeare's collaborator, John Fletcher, but this usually won't matter for audition.

He could be any age you care above about mid-twenties.

---

1   *intemperate surfeit of her eye* over-indulgence in gazing (at Palamon)
      distempered unbalanced
2–3 *execute their preordained faculties* work normally
3–4 *in a most extravagant vagary* wandering wildly (The latter words both come from the Latin 'vagari', which means 'to wander'.)
4   *you* (i.e. the Wooer.)
7   *commune* talk intimately
8   *beats upon* is obsessed by
9–10 *pranks and friskins* practical jokes and frolickings
10   *green* youthful
11   *stuck in* decorated with
13   *compounded odours* blended perfumes
14   *grateful to the sense* pleasing to the sense (of smell)
      become be consistent with
16   *carve her* serve her (food, as a high-born lady)
      still among every now and then (along with these other activities)
19   *playferes* playmates
      repair to visit
20   *as if they suggested for him* which make her think of him
21   *falsehood* delusion
22   *bring* induce
      reduce restore
23   *out of square* abnormal
24   *regiment* orderly state
      approved demonstrated (that this treatment works)
26   *passages* proceedings
27   *appliance* remedy (He's probably hinting at his idea for that which will finally cure her.)

Act 4, Scene 3
Doctor –

1   That intemperate surfeit of her eye hath distempered the other senses. They may return and settle again to execute their preordained faculties, but they are now in a most extravagant vagary. This you must do: confine her to a place where the
5   light may rather seem to steal in than be permitted; take upon you, young sir her friend, the name of Palamon; say you come to eat with her and to commune of love. This will catch her attention, for this her mind beats upon – other objects that are inserted 'tween her mind and eye become the pranks and
10   friskins of her madness. Sing to her such green songs of love as she says Palamon hath sung in prison. Come to her stuck in as sweet flowers as the season is mistress of, and thereto make an addition of some other compounded odours which are grateful to the sense. All this shall become Palamon, for
15   Palamon can sing, and Palamon is sweet and every good thing. Desire to eat with her, carve her, drink to her, and still among intermingle your petition of grace and acceptance into her favour. Learn what maids have been her companions and playferes, and let them repair to her with Palamon in their
20   mouths, and appear with tokens as if they suggested for him. It is a falsehood she is in, which is with falsehoods to be combated. This may bring her to eat, to sleep, and reduce what's now out of square in her into their former law and regiment. I have seen it approved, how many times I know
25   not, but to make the number more I have great hope in this. I will, between the passages of this project, come in with my appliance. Let us put it in execution, and hasten the success,
28   which doubt not will bring forth comfort.   *Exeunt*

The Winter's Tale

Leontes

Leontes is the King of Sicilia and husband of Hermione. Polixenes, King of Bohemia and his friend since childhood, who has been staying at Leontes' court for nine months, has not long said that he must return home tomorrow. Leontes suggests he stays another week. At first Polixenes refuses but Hermione manages persuade him. However, in the course of their discussion, Leontes perceives an undue intimacy between them and becomes extremely jealous, convinced that they have been having an affair. Whilst Hermione and Polixenes talk apart, Leontes muses angrily to himself and then calls his son, Mamillius, and asks playfully, 'Art thou my calf?' His son replies, 'Yes, if you will my lord.' Leontes continues with this speech.

From his demeanour Mamillius is probably about seven; he was born when his father was twenty-three, so Leontes is probably about thirty.

---

1   *rough pash* shaggy head
    shoots horns (i.e. of the grown bull and the symbol of the cuckold.)
2   *full* entirely
5   *o'er-dyed blacks* (i.e. black clothes made of fragile material through over-dyeing – it was then very difficult and expensive to manufacture a deep black cloth.)
7   *bourn* boundary
9   *welkin* blue (like the sky)
10   *collop* a small piece of meat (As in 'My own flesh and blood.')
    dam mother
11   *Affection* (i.e. Sexual desire.)
    intention intensity
    centre heart
12   *not so held* not supposed possible
15   *fellow'st nothing* you associate yourself with what doesn't exist
    credent credible
17   *commission* that which is authorized
    find experience

Act 1, Scene 2
Leontes –

1   Thou want'st a rough pash and the shoots that I have,
     To be full like me. Yet they say we are
     Almost as like as eggs. Women say so,
     That will say anything. But were they false
5   As o'er-dyed blacks, as wind, as waters; false
     As dice are to be wished by one that fixes
     No bourn 'twixt his and mine; yet were it true
     To say this boy were like me. Come, sir page,
     Look on me with your welkin eye. Sweet villain,
10   Most dear'st, my collop! Can thy dam – may 't be? –
     Affection, thy intention stabs the centre.
     Thou dost make possible things not so held,
     Communicat'st with dreams – how can this be? –
     With what's unreal thou coactive art,
15   And fellow'st nothing. Then 'tis very credent
     Thou mayst co-join with something, and thou dost –
     And that beyond commission; and I find it –
     And that to the infection of my brains
19   And hard'ning of my brows.

The Winter's Tale

The Clown

The Clown (we are never told his name) is the son of a Shepherd; both of whom are part of a group of country people who inhabit Bohemia and feature in the second half of the play. There has been a terrible storm; father and son have been calling urgently to each other across the landscape. The Clown has just found his father, who ask him: 'What ail'st thou, man?' This is his reply.

Later in the play he is seen as a kind, fun-loving, generous, but gullible young man. The name 'Clown' is nowadays somewhat misleading as he does not consciously set out to be comic. He is funny to us through his innocence of the ways of the world and his enthusiasms. At the end of this scene he goes off to bury Antigonus, 'if there be any of him left'.

In the second half of the play – sixteen years after this event – he seems to be in his twenties. Therefore he could be played as a child in this speech.

I have edited several speeches together to create this speech.

---

1   *such* incredible
1–2 *am not* to cannot
3   *bodkin's* needle's
5   *takes* swallows
8   *yeast* foam (This is 'yest' in some editions.)
9   *hogshead* a very large container for liquids
10   *land-service* events on shore (Literally, military service on land, in contrast to that at sea.)
12   *make an end of* finish (the story of)
13   *flap-dragoned* swallowed fast (Flap-dragons were raisins floating in burning brandy which were caught in the mouth, still alight, and extinguished.)
16–17 *I have not winked since* It was only a moment

Act 3, Scene 3
Clown –

1   I have seen two such sights, by sea and by land! But I am
not to say it is a sea, for it is now the sky: betwixt the
firmament and it you cannot thrust a bodkin's point. I
would you did but see how it chafes, how it rages, how it
5   takes up the shore – but that's not to the point! O, the
most piteous cry of the poor souls! Sometimes to see 'em,
and not to see 'em; now the ship boring the moon with
her mainmast, and anon swallowed with yeast and froth,
as you'd thrust a cork into a hogshead. And then for the
10   land-service: to see how the bear tore out his shoulder-
bone, how he cried to me for help, and said his name was
Antigonus, a nobleman! But to make an end of the ship –
to see how the sea flap-dragoned it! But first, how the
poor souls roared, and the sea mocked them; and how the
15   poor gentleman roared, and the bear mocked him, both
roaring louder than the sea or weather. I have not winked
since I saw these sights. The men are not yet cold under
water, nor the bear half dined on the gentleman. He's at it
19   now.

Bibliography

The Plays

I referred to the Arden, New Penguin, Oxford, Peter Alexander and Riverside editions and found different aspects to recommend each of them. If I am to recommend one particular edition – for actors – I would marginally recommend the Oxford editions. *The Complete Works* (General Editors: Stanley Wells & Gary Taylor) were published in 1988 by Oxford University Press, and the individual plays are appearing in paperback with some excellent notes.

Shakespeare Reference

Charles Boyce, *Shakespeare – The Essential Reference to His Plays, His Poems, His Life, And More* (Roundtable Press)

Peter Quennell and Hamish Johnson, *Who's Who in Shakespeare* (Routledge, 1996)

About Shakespeare and His Plays

There are an impossible number of books on this subject; the ones I've got most out of are:

Anthony Burgess, *Shakespeare* (Penguin, 1970) – this is not a history book but a wonderful evocation of who Shakespeare might have been and how he might have lived his life.

A. L. Rowse, *Shakespeare the Elizabethan* (Weidenfeld & Nicholson, 1977) – although written by an eminent academic historian, this is a good read.

Jan Kott, *Shakespeare Our Contemporary* (W.W. Norton & Company, 1964) – although he writes about only a few of the plays, the author gives a wonderful evocation of Shakespeare in our time.

About Acting and Auditioning

Uta Hagen, *A Challenge for the Actor* (Macmillan, 1991) – the best book on acting ever written.

Simon Dunmore, *An Actor's Guide to Getting Work* (A&C Black, 2001) – all you need to know about auditioning and all aspects of being an actor.

Simon Dunmore, *Alternative Shakespeare Auditions for Men* (A&C Black, 1997) – my first collection of fifty speeches.

Ellis Jones, *Teach Yourself Acting* (Hodder & Stoughton Ltd., 1998) – a good overview of acting and the profession.